Claudia Stein

Tel Aviv 2015
The Retro Travel Guide.

Production and Publishing:Create Space
ISBN-13: 978-1494225575
ISBN-10: 1494225573

1st edition

Disclaimer:
I disclaim any responsibility for the information given throughout this book. I did my very best to provide accurate information, and I cannot assume any responsibility for mistakes or changes that might occur.
Claudia Stein

Table Of Contents

Preface

Tel Aviv. This is where modernity merges with Levantine traditions; the city celebrated its 100th birthday in 2009 and is home to the world's most extensive collection of buildings designed in the International Style. The history of the Jewish immigrants who followed their vision of a Jewish state that would give them protection and unite the Jewish people can still be traced.

Since the publication of the first edition of this Guide (June 2012) much has happened in Tel Aviv: the bus companies have improved their network and the tariffs; the city administration has expanded the tourist information center, there is more public wi-fi in the city, etc. ... But also international recognition has not long in coming. Tel Aviv became part of the 28 cities that form the UNESCO Creative Cities Network. The award honors the local firms' creativity and innovation that shape life in Tel Aviv so much more than in any other city. Although the city has only 400,000 inhabitants, more than 700 start-ups in the early stages can be counted. So it is no wonder that Tel Aviv has prevailed in November 2014 against 250 international competitors and was honored as "Smartest City" for its investment in a digital future.

This travel guide invites you to beautiful beaches, historical witnesses, fascinating architecture, cultural fusion of Orient and Occident and the busy nightlife of Tel Aviv, the city that never stops.

Tel Aviv, April 2015,
Claudia Stein

1   In A Nutshell

1.1   Israel

Official Name: Medinat Yisrael = State of Israel

Telephone Country Code: +972, mobile phones +972-5

Internet: .co.il

Time Zone: UTC +2

Currency: New Israeli Shekel (NIS), 1 NIS = 100 Agorot, ca. 0.20 EUR.

Founding of State: 5 Iyar 5708 (14 May 1948)

Form of Government: Parliamentary republic

National Independence Holiday: 5. Iyar

Capital and Seat of Government: Jerusalem

Official Languages: Modern Hebrew (Ivrit), Arabic

Population: ca. 8.18 Mio (May 2014)

Area: 22,072 km² / 8,522 mi² (without autonomous regions)

Religions: Judaism (75.3%), Islam (20.5 %), other (4.2%)

National Anthem: HaTikwa (Eng.: "The Hope")

Biggest City: Jerusalem (ca. 775,000 residents)

1.2   Short Bio of Tel Aviv

Official Name: Tel Aviv-Yafo

Telephone City Code: 03

Founded: 11 April 1909 as Achuzat Beit

Area: 51.4 km² / 19.9 mi², metropolitan area: 1,516 km² / 585 mi²

* Population: ca. 400,000 (city center), ca. 3.3 million (metropolitan area)

Religions (municipal area): Judaism 91%, Islam 3%, Christianity 1%, other 5%

Mayor: Ron Huldai (since 1998)

*For comparison:

Berlin 890 km² (343 mi²), New York 1,213 km² (468 mi²), Paris 105 km² (40.7 mi²)

2 General Information

2.1 Security in Israel

In today's political climate where terrorism is a general concern in nearly every place of the world, how safe a trip to Israel will be is difficult to say. Israelis are very aware of the threats and have high-level safety measures in place: there is no shopping mall, bus station or parking lot where bags or the trunk of a car will not be inspected; even at the supermarkets you have to open your bag to the security staff (unlike other countries where the concern is much bigger about what you take out than what you bring in.) Basic rule of thumb: stay away from the borders; you might get involved in conflicts even though you were not the target. There are more ways to get to the Red Sea than along the Egyptian border. The Gaza strip is really a heavily contested area, and it would be extremely ill-advised to include it in your sightseeing plans. It would be best not to even get close as the rockets from Gaza to Israel have become part of daily life in that area, unfortunately. If you really have to visit the West Bank, it will be much safer to go together with a local person. Remember: if something happens to you in these territories, even your embassy might not be able to help. It is always good to call them before you go there and inquire about the current situation. Beware of the opening hours of the borders! Border checkpoints are also subject to closing without prior notice for security reasons. Crossing the border with an Israeli car is risky; you are a target while a foreign car in Israel is not of concern. Your car rental agreement might already waive the possibility to visit other countries with this car. It is also better to drive during the daytime.

An unattended piece of luggage is always of great concern. If you discover one, please tell a local person about it.

2.2 Emergency Numbers

Tel Aviv is a vibrant cosmopolitan city, and you should not do anything you would not do anywhere else. Common sense is all you need in this city, which is not more dangerous than Paris or Madrid, actually less. Foreign tourists are considered easy victims all around the world and especially women might think twice about how much they show, just like elsewhere in the Middle East. In the unlikely case that something happens to you, and you have access to a phone, these are the emergency numbers to call (only work from Israeli phones):

- police: 100
- ambulance: 101
- fire department: 102

2.3   Health Care and Emergencies

Israeli hospitals have a very good reputation. If you urgently need a doctor during your stay in Tel Aviv, you can go to the Sourasky Medical Center (the former Ichilov General Hospital.) This highly modern center is home to three different hospitals and is one of the best in the country. Normally, you have to pay for the treatment right away at the site, and all credit cards are accepted. If it is not an emergency, your embassy can provide you with a list of doctors who speak your language.

2.3.1   Hospitals and Clinics

1) Tel Aviv Sourasky Medical Center
Weizman St. 10,
Tel. 03-697.4444,
http://www.tasmc.org.il

2) This dental clinic is open 24/7:
Zeitlin St. 1 / Ecke Ibn Gvirol,
Tel. 03-691.5951
http://www.telavivdental.com/

2.3.2   Pharmacies

There are plenty of pharmacies all over Tel Aviv, and you will not have a hard time finding one except for Shabbat (Saturday) and holidays. The following place belongs to the pharmacy chain SuperPharm and is open on Shabbat from 08.00 to 20.00 hours (no guarantee.) You can also consult the English edition of the local newspapers, like the Jerusalem Post, to see, which place is on duty.

3) Dizengoff St. 129 / Gordon St.

2.4 Good to know!

2.4.1 Immigration

Tourists need a passport that is still valid for at least six months from the date of their departure. For tourists from many countries, there is no need to apply for a prearranged visa, and visitors are allowed to stay in the country for up to three months. Please consult with the Israeli Embassy to determine if your country participates in the Visa Waiver Program. Holders of non-machine readable passports will always need a prearranged visa, however. If you want to stay longer in Israel, you can apply for an extension at the Israeli Ministry of Internal Affairs. Information is available on their website: http://mfa.gov.il/mfa/Pages/default.aspx

2.4.2 Departure

Please make sure you are at the airport at least 3 hours before departure. Due to high-level security measures you will be interviewed about your stay before check-in, the luggage will be x-rayed and many times also manually inspected.

If you fly home with a low-cost airline, the schedule might be really tight, and you have to calculate at least three hours lead time. At the moment, the check-in is located in the old terminal, but the flights are leaving from terminal 3. If you come to the airport by train, you will arrive in terminal 3, then you have to take a shuttle to terminal 1 and after check-in another shuttle back to terminal 3 from where all international flights are departing. The shuttle runs only every 15 minutes. Perhaps you will take the return flight prefer a taxi to the airport.

Ben-Gurion-Airport
Tel. (03) 972 3333
www.iaa.gov.il

2.4.3 Official Tourist Information

The city hall is now operating two offices in the city.

1.) City Center (at the beach promenade, close to Allenby St.)
Herbert Samuel St. 46 / Geula St. 1 November - 31 March: Su.-Th. 09.30-17.30, Fr. 09.00-13.00, 1 April - 31 October: Su.-Th. 09.30-18.30, Fr. 09.00-13.00
2.) Jaffa (at the roundabout traffic, close to Clock Tower)
Marzuk ve Azar St. 2, 1 November - 31 March: Su.-Th. 09.30-17.30, Fr. 09.30-14.00, 1 April - 31 October: Su.-Th. 09.30-18.30, Fr. 09.30-14.00, Sa. 10.00-16.00

Tel. (03) 516.6188
http://www.visit-tlv.com

2.4.4   Embassies

3) Embassy of the United States
HaYarkon St. 71
Tel. 03-519.7475

4) Embassy of the UK
Ben Yehuda St. 1
Tel. 03-725.1222

5.) Embassy of Canada
Nirim St. 3/ 5
Tel. 03-636.3300

2.4.5   Money

Credit cards are widely accepted for almost any purchase. Most ATMs show the display in Hebrew and switch to English the moment you enter a foreign credit card.

2.4.6   Telephone

Th City/Area Code of Tel Aviv is 03 (from abroad or a foreign mobile phone, +972-3) and Israeli mobile phone numbers start with 05. If your mobile phone accepts foreign SIM cards, you might consider getting an Israeli prepaid SIM card once you are in the country. The cost of making calls from a local Israeli mobile phone number while in Israel (via an Israeli SIM card installed in your mobile phone) will be considerably less than making them using your home country's SIM card and paying for international roaming charges. In most supermarkets, you can recharge your prepaid SIM card at the cash desk.

2.5 Holidays

The official calendar in Israel is the Jewish calendar. If you are free in your planning, the following holidays might be worth taking into account. For Israelis, it is so natural that there are reduced opening hours already the day before the holiday, they simply forget to tell the tourists about it (e.g. when you want to pick up your car in a location other than the airport.)

The most important rule is this: Jewish days start in the evening, including the holidays (see Genesis 1:5: "And there was evening and there was morning, one day.") Consequently, Shabbat starts already on Friday evening. The evening when the holiday starts is called erev (evening) + name of the holiday; that turns Friday evening into erev Shabbat. The correct greetings on a holiday and on Shabbat are *hag sameah* and *Shabbat shalom*, respectively.

Shabbat

taxi: yes, pt: no

On the seventh day the Creator decided to rest and this is how the Jews still do it today. Shabbat is by law a holiday in Israel. Tel Aviv is a very secular city and unlike Jerusalem, many places are open except state-owned or public institutions which normally close on Friday around 14.00. The public transport shuts down during Friday afternoon until Saturday late afternoon / evening. Taxis and Sherut (shared taxis) do operate on Shabbat.

For religious Jews, Shabbat is not just the weekend. On Friday evening the "bride Shabbat" is welcome in the synagogue and next morning, in the presence of at least 10 male Jews, the Torah scrolls are taken out to read the weekly Torah portion. It is a special day where people dress well, spend time with their family, have a nice dinner together and study the Torah. Shabbat ends after dusk. Sunday is the first day of the week and everybody is back to work.

Rosh HaShana (Jewish New Year)

1 Tishrei (September/October), taxi yes, pt: no

The Jewish year starts in fall and from 1 Tishrei on, a marathon of holidays takes place, the High Holidays. The ten days from the New Year to Yom Kippur are also called the Days of Awe; atonement and repentance are the main themes. This time of year is very busy in Israel. Many Israelis take holidays to visit their families, Jews living abroad come to Israel for the same reason. The roads are busy and traveling in Israel can be a bit more exhausting than normal. The correct greeting for the Jewish New Year is *Shaná Tová*.

Yom Kippur (Day of Atonement)
10 Tishrei (September/October) taxi, pt, music: no
Nothing happens on Yom Kippur. NOTHING. Life stands still, including at the airport and the borders. There is no TV and no radio. Not even taxis or any other vehicle are allowed to drive in the streets that day (except fire department and ambulance.) Secular Jews make the best out of it by enjoying the freedom to cycle on the motorway.

The *Days of Awe* are a very serious matter. According to the Jewish faith, everybody's destiny is written in a book on the New Year, but this "book of life" will not be sealed before Yom Kippur. In those ten days people are forgiven for everything they have done wrong against G"d and against others. The day of Yom Kippur is spent nearly entirely in synagogue services and after 25 hours of fasting, the end of this holiday is celebrated with a rich dinner.

Sukkot (Feast of Tabernacles)
15 Tishrei (September/October), taxi yes, pt: no
It is one of the three Pilgrimage Festivals (later in the Jewish calendar there is also Pesah and Shavuot.) During the course of history, this festival has changed significantly. In the times of the temple, the first fruits of the harvest were sacrificed on Sukkot. After the temple was destroyed, this tradition could not be continued. Today, Sukkot (Hebrew: sukká = hut, sukkót = huts) reminds us of the time of deprivation on the way to the Holy Land. Religious Jews build a sukká in their garden or on their balcony and take all their meals in there. Many even spend the night in them. Most of the Jewish congregations, especially abroad, have one big sukká for their congregants.

Sukkot (Feast of Tabernacles)
15 Tishrei (September/October), taxi yes, pt: no
It is one of the three Pilgrimage Festivals (later in the Jewish calendar there is also Pesah and Shavuot.) During the course of history, this festival has changed significantly. In the times of the temple, the first fruits of the harvest were sacrificed on Sukkot. After the temple was destroyed, this tradition could not be continued. Today, Sukkot (Hebrew: *sukká* = hut, *sukkót* = huts) reminds us of the time of deprivation on the way to the Holy Land. Religious Jews build a *sukká* in their garden or on their balcony and take all their meals in there. Many even spend the night in them. Most of the Jewish congregations, especially abroad, have one big sukká for their congregants.

Hanukah

25 Kislev (November/December) taxi: yes, pt: yes

The Hanukah celebrations will be a rather enriching experience for tourists rather than a handicap in their travel planning. During the eight days of Hanukah, you will see Hanukah candleholders everywhere (sometimes they are permanent installations) and people eat doughnuts (in Hebrew: *sufganyot*), and hash browns (in Yiddish: *lattkes*.) With oily meals the Jews remember for 8 days the Revolt of the Maccabees in 164 BCE that had led to the re-dedication of the Temple in Jerusalem, formerly desecrated by the Greeks. When they entered the Temple, they found a very small quantity of sacred oil left but it lasted for eight days until new oil had been made.

Purim

14 Adar (in Jerusalem on 15 Adar, March) taxi yes, pt: yes

If you like Carnival, costumes and theme parties… this is your holiday! All over town you will find Purim parties and people wearing costumes. The biblical book of Esther tells the story of Purim, the salvation of the Jews from the Persian diaspora by Queen Esther who successfully stopped the murder of the Jewish people through Haman (Xerxe's governmental official in the Persian Empire) who had fixed the day by lot (Hebrew: pur = lot, purim = lots.) Alcohol and lots of pastries, "oznai haman" (Haman's ears) or "haman tashen" are part of the celebrations.

Pesah (Exodus from Egypt)

15 Nissan (March/April) taxi: yes, pt: no

The second of the three Pilgrimage Festivals might be a little bit more difficult to digest for tourists, though in Tel Aviv many residents simply ignore the prohibition on selling leavened bread and are ready to accept the fine. During this week no cereal product is supposed to be offered, including beer. The traditional Matsot look like crisp bread but with even less taste. The big fast food chains use cornmeal during this week, others just do not sell any kind of bakery products or simply close and go on vacation. There will also be a much reduced offer for anything that is eaten with pita bread like shavarma and falafel.

This holiday remembers the exodus of the Jewish people from Egypt and the salvation from slavery. There was no time left to bake bread for the journey and for this reason bread and cereals are banned from the kitchen for one week. The first evening is normally spent with family. Together they have a traditional meal that is eaten in a certain order and the "Haggada" is read (the religious book on the exodus from Egypt.)

Yom HaAtzmaut (Independence Day)

5 Iyar (April/May) taxi yes, pt: yes

Independence Day (pronounced: Yom Ha-Atzma-Oot) is one of the best times to be in Tel Aviv: beach parties, open-air concerts, decorated balconies... everybody is in a party mood. The official celebrations take place in Jerusalem and can be followed on huge screens. The State of Israel was founded on 5 Iyar 5708 (14 May 1948) in Tel Aviv on Rothschild Boulevard No. 16.

On the day before (called Yom HaSikaron, Memorial Day), Israel traditionally commemorates the killed Israeli soldiers. In order to make sure that this day is never on Shabbat, in some years it is artificially moved to another date and so is Independence Day. Another holiday that cannot be on Shabbat is Yom HaShoa, the Holocaust Memorial Day (27 Nissan / April.) On Yom HaSikaron and Yom HaShoa, sirens sound throughout the country. Everything and everybody will stop, even cars and buses, to commemorate the dead. For one minute, nothing else seems to matter. Israelis expect tourists to do the same.

!!! In the evening of Yom HaSikaron, Yom HaShoa and Yom Kippur (remember: **holidays start in the evening**,) all cafés and restaurants are closed. No exception. taxi, pt, music: no

2.5.1 Holidays 2015/ 2016

Purim 04 March 2015/ 23 March 2016

Pesach 03 April 2015/ 22 April 2016

Yom HaAtzmaut 22 April 2015/ 11 May 2016

Rosh HaShana: 13 September 2015/ 02 October 2016

Yom Kipur: 22 September 2015/ 11 October 2016

Sukkot 27 September 2015/ 16 October 2016

Simchat Thora 04 October 2015/ 23 October 2016

Channuka 06 December 2015/ 24 December 2016

2.6 Yearly Events

February
* Jazz Festival http://www.jazzfest.co.il/

March/ April
* Días de Flamenco http://www.keren-adi.org
* Marathon Tel Aviv http://www.tlvmarathon.co.il

May

- Felicja Blumental International Music Festival
  http://www.blumentalfestival.com
- Houses from Within http://www.batim-il.org

June

- Tel Aviv Pride, White Night Festival
- Student Film Festival http://www.taufilmfest.com
  Tel Aviv LGBT Film Festival http://www.tlvfest.com

July

- Opera in the Park http://www.israel-opera.co.il
- Madridanza Tel Aviv http://www.suzannedellal.org.il

September

- Loving Art Making Art

October

- SPIRIT Film Festival http://www.spiritfestival.co.il
- Tel Aviv Dance http://www.israel-opera.co.il

November

- Curtain Up Dance Festival http://www.suzannedellal.org.il

2.7   For Everybody: Israeli Folk Dances at the Beach

The Association of Israeli Folk Dances meets almost every week at Gordon Beach for a public dancing. Participation is welcome and free of charge. The dates can be found online under "Saturday's Free Dance Sessions": http://www.harokdim.org/indexENG.php.

2.8   Public Transport

First things first: on Shabbat there is no public transport, except mini-vans and taxis. On Friday afternoons just before Shabbat, buses and trains stop operating. Make sure you get to your destination early. During late afternoon / early evening on Saturday, the transport company is back to work.

After your arrival, you can choose between taxi and train to get to Tel Aviv, but there is a considerable difference in price between the two options (e.g. ca. 16 NIS for train and ca. 140 NIS for taxi.) Even though it is very easy to travel around Israel by bus, some places like natural parks or remote beaches can only be reached by car. In comparison to other countries, cars can be rented at reasonable prices in Israel.

2.8.1   Taxi

Tourists should use only the official taxis and make sure the meter is switched on, but this is usually not a problem. Of course, you can negotiate the price with the driver beforehand. The distance between airport and city center Tel Aviv, like Dizengoff Square, will cost you around 140 NIS depending on the traffic. For single travelers, the best deal is the train. When you are leaving Tel Aviv, you can take a taxi or bus to the next train station and then go to the airport by train for ca. 15 NIS. Since there are only shared taxis between Jerusalem and the airport but not from or to Tel Aviv, it is easy to find somebody at the airport who is more than happy to share the ride with you.

!!! In Israel it is not customary to tip taxi drivers.

2.8.2   Bus

Public busses are quite cheap; a single ticket costs less than 6 NIS. The ticket can be bought from the bus driver. You can choose between a single ticket or a multi-ride ticket (kartisiyá). A 10-ride ticket for one zone (all Tel Aviv) costs less than 50 NIS. The rides will be saved on a plastic card (rav-kav) which you buy once for 5 NIS. The card is valid for eight years and can be used by several people.

With each ticket you can ride for 90 minutes within the city and also change bus lines. The bus tickets do not work for the mini buses. If you are in the city for longer and think about getting a monthly pass, you will have to get an individual rav-kav card with your photo on it. These cards are issued in the offices from the bus lines, e.g. in the New Central Bus Station on Levinsky Street. On the 6th and 7th floor of this not very inviting looking shopping center you will find the offices of EGGED (pronounced e-gedd) and DAN, respectively.

All pre-purchased multi-ride tickets get always saved on the plastic card. This is even possible for different cities. A maximum of eight different tickets can be stored on the same card at the same time.

Tel Aviv and the neighboring cities belong to "Zone 1", except for Herzliya. With one tariff you can travel quite far, including Rishon Le Zion in the south and Ganei Tikva in the east. Just behind the northern part of Tel Aviv, Ramat Aviv, "Zone 21" starts and a ticket to Herzliya is a bit more expensive than one to Rishon Le Zion.

2.8.3 Sherut

Sherut means service. This is the name for the mini vans that run from north to south through the city as shared taxis. You can stop them anywhere, not only at the bus station and you can get off any time you like. They also run on Shabbat and late at night.

2.8.4 Train

Sherut means service. This is the name for the mini-vans that run from north to south through the city as shared taxis. You can stop them anywhere, not only at the bus station, and you can get off any time you like. They also run on Shabbat and late at night. A single ticket to the airport costs 16 NIS. The train operates from 05.00 a.m. to 0.30 a.m, except for Shabbat (Friday 03.00 p.m. to Saturday evening about 09.00 p.m).

2.8.5 Car

This is a special subject: driving. Israel holds a stable position in the world's "top ten" countries for mortal road accidents. The speed limit of 100 km / h on the motorway seems still too high for the Israeli way of driving: Israeli drivers maintain virtually no distance between the cars and the turn signal is only used by newbies and foreigners.

For most tourists, the gasoline stations are a real surprise. In many places you have to go to the cash desk first to make them unlock the gas pump and depending on the oil company, a foreign credit card may only be accepted for up to 200 NIS. If it is not a self-service place, the attendant will type your license number into the computer and ask "Malé?" (full?).

2.8.6 Rental Car

As long as you stay in Tel Aviv, having a car is a very painful experience most of the time since parking facilities are not abundant and there are no meters in the street. As a tourist, you will likely end up with a ticket. You might be well advised to not pick up your car too early when you plan on leaving town.

The rental companies at the airport provide a shuttle service to their parking lots. If you decide to not give back the car at the airport, make sure you ask when picking up the car where exactly it should be dropped off – signs are sometimes rare – and what the opening hours will be at that day. If the next day is a holiday, the office might close earlier than usual. Only the offices at the airport are 24/7.

2.8.7 Parking

In recent years, a car-park routing system has been installed. If you prefer to park your car in the street, you might want to bear in mind this basic rule: if the curb is red, keep driving. It does not matter whether it is red-white, red-yellow or red-gray. Parking could be permitted next to the red-gray area but you have to be able to read the sign with all the exceptions, the same for blue-white. In any case, it is not for free. The municipality has developed a very sophisticated system of display tickets without installing any individual-space parking meters in the street. From 17.00 onward, parking in the street is theoretically only allowed for residents. If you remain parked beyond this time, chances are you will be fined.

2.8.8 Bike

Tel Aviv has only a few bike paths, but biking is very enjoyable here! In no time you can be anywhere in the city and the scenery is amazing. Since 2011, Tel Aviv provides a public bike rental system, Tel-O-Fun. The green bikes are parked all over the city and the system is also open to non-residents. The terminals are also in English and accept foreign credit cards. Alternatively, you can rent a bike from a private rental place. The latter has one advantage that is reflected in the price: you can come back any time and change the bike or if you have any other problem. Even when the bike has to be replaced after a theft, it is cheaper in a private place than at the city hall.

Some suggestions for bike rental:

Tel-O-Fun

Tel-O-Fun belongs to the municipality and provides rental bikes virtually "around every corner" of the city. The price is a combination of membership (min. 1 day) and rental time. The locations can be found on their website where they also show videos in different languages on how to use the service.
https://www.tel-o-fun.co.il/en/
http://www.youtube.com/user/telofun

O-Fun-Bikes is a friendly bike shop with rental service. Their team speaks very good English and they offer different types of bikes. The rental price includes a thick chain with a lock and also a helmet. They also rent child seats and tandem bikes.
!!! Closes Friday at 2.00 pm until Sunday 10.00!!!

1.) Ben Yehuda St. 197, Tel. 03-544.2292, Su.-Th. 10.00-19.00, Fr. 10.00-14.00, http://o-fun.co.il/

At **Cycle Tel Aviv** you can even rent those trailers with which you can dock a kid's bike onto your own and make a tandem. This way you can cycle together safely through the city.

2.) Ben Yehuda St. 147, Tel. 03-529.3037, Su.-Th. 10.00-19.00, Fr. 10.00-15.00, http://cycle.co.il/

Mopeds or motor bikes can be rented from **MotoGo**:
3.) Tushia St. 19-21, Tel. 3-681.1717, http://www.motogo.co.il

3   Urban History

The official name of the city is Tel Aviv-Yafo. This little hyphen connects more than just two words, it connects two different worlds with painful memories. The history of ancient Jaffa can well be traced until the 19th century. Much less was documented in the last 150-200 years and many of those documents only exist in Arabic, which means that most people in the western world have no access to this information. The research of the history of Tel Aviv was also a challenge to the historians but for very different reasons. The history of the city, which many claim it does not even have, is shrouded in mystery. Legend has it that it was a suburb of Jaffa that miraculously became a metropolitan city over the years. Others say that Tel Aviv had been built by German Jews who fled Nazi Germany, hence all the Bauhaus buildings. There are many other versions around but so far, none has told the historical facts or considered the political environment of that time which shows the founding of the city in a totally new and even more impressive perspective.

Only in the last 10-15 years have historians, architects and city planners – Israelis and foreigners –started searching for the traces of the city and its origins. The wish to get the architecture recognized by UNESCO (achieved in 2003) reinforced the need for documentation. At the beginning of the 20th century there were many languages spoken in the area — English, Hebrew, German, Yiddish, Russian and Arabic — and therefore, all documents that were finally found were in different languages. Arabic was mainly used to purchase land from wealthy Arabic owners who mostly did not even live in Palestine and to whom those sand dunes were of little value. The political changes had added another burden to the project. Old maps were the hardest to find and if found, to categorize. Maps and documents from the period of the British Mandate (1918-1948) have practically completely disappeared or had been moved from Tel Aviv to Jerusalem and nobody has ever found them again. At the same time, it was customary to change street names and personal names to Hebrew. Still today, new immigrants are allowed to change their names once they come to Israel. There are still doubts in many cases if two names on different documents refer to the same person or not.

3.1   Jaffa

According to one of the many legends, Jaffa was founded by Yophet (Arabic: Yafet), one of the three sons of Noah and one of the eight survivors of the Noachian flood. The exact year is not documented. Excavations have shown that there are eight different settlements below the Jaffa we know it today, witnesses of roughly 3,800 years of history. It is yet unclear who those settlers were but they were not the same during the whole time; for the last 4,000 years people were moving in and out. The harbor of Jaffa had turned the city into a regional economic center from its earliest years. It had brought the city wealth and international trade relations.

Already early in its history, the natural harbor turned Jaffa into an important economic center in the region. The city became rich, cosmopolitan and also the desire of all rulers at that time. The Canaanites, the Philistines, King David and his son King Salomon, Napoleon and the Ottomans – they all had an eye on Jaffa. At the end of the 13th century ACE, after successfully defeating the Crusaders at the harbor, the Mamelukes destroyed the harbor to prevent their enemies from coming back. The Ottomans captured Palestine at the beginning of the 16th century and controlled it until Napoleon arrived in 1799. The area increased in prosperity and the harbor was renewed. During this period numerous Christian pilgrims arrived by boat in Jaffa on their way to Jerusalem. When Egyptian Muhammad Ali Pasha conquered Jaffa, wealthy Egyptian families decided to immigrate. In the following years, Jews from Northern Africa and Turkey also found their way to Jaffa. Slowly but steadily, Jewish life came back again. Those Jews who had already been in the country for quite some time belonged to the Sephardim. Their ancestors had fled from Spain and Portugal and their lifestyle was very oriental. The Ashkenazim – from Middle and Eastern Europe – had not been in the country before ca. 1840. Most could not maintain themselves, lived mainly for the study of the Torah and were dependant on payments from the diaspora. When the Ottomans defeated Muhammad Ali Pasha in 1841, Jaffa became an economic center once more. The construction of the Jaffa light house in 1865 was very foresightful: only 4 years later in 1869, the Suez Canal opened and Jaffa became even more important, soon even indispensible: the growing production of Jaffa oranges were exported to many countries.

In the meantime (September 1866) George Jones Adams, founder of the "Church of the Messiah," and his 156 followers had come from Boston to Jaffa. They bought a plot of land, erected the wooden prefabricated houses they had brought from home and started a community in the north of Jaffa that can still be seen today around Bar Hoffman Street. None of them had been prepared for the hardship of agricultural life abroad and only a few months later, in winter 1867 most of them wanted to leave Jaffa and go back home. The majority of them had already left when in the beginning of 1869 some Southern German "Templers" arrived and offered to buy from Adams' group their settlement that would later be known as the "(American-) German Colony of Jaffa." The Templers founded a new settlement east of Jaffa in 1871, Sarona. At the same time there were plans to open a railway connection from Jaffa to Jerusalem and in 1888, the Templers added another little compound close to the future train station. The railway line was opened in 1892. The construction of the railway confirmed Jaffa's status and brought even more business activities to the city.

The old train station, "HaTachana," was renovated a couple of years ago and is a nice and lively place with coffee shops, restaurants and boutiques today. The train station was located in the former urban Arabic quarter of Manshiye that was demolished in the 1960s. In 1870s the first sections of the old city wall were torn down to prepare for future expansion. A new urban district developed in the north of Jaffa, right next to the beach: Manshiye. The Charles Clore Park stands on the former western part of this quarter. The Jewish citizens of Jaffa moved further north and founded Neve Tzedek, Hebrew for "Oasis of Justice," (1887) and Neve Shalom, Hebrew for "Oasis of Peace" (1890.) The stand-alone Etzel Museum is one of the last witnesses to history as well as the train station itself, the Red House next to it and last but not least the Hassan Bek Mosque. After the demolition the municipality had planned to erect the Tel Aviv Business District here. But these plans were later abandoned and today the business district can be found at the border of Ramat Gan, next to the Ayalon Highway. Other new quarters from this time are Ajami and Jabaliya in the south and Souza and Salameh in the east. It was a time of a blossoming economy and more foreigners from many different countries would immigrate. The Maronite and Coptic Christians started to populate Ajami where you can still today find many churches built in those days.

In summer 1914 Hassan Bek became the new mayor of Jaffa and the mosque of Manshiye – built in 1916 – bears his name. Bek had a vision; he wanted to modernize the country and the big and wide Boulevards the Europeans had introduced to the Middle East served him as a model. After the break-out of World War I he expelled all Russian citizens from Jaffa. Russia was the arch-enemy of Turkey and Bek feared conflicts in Jaffa. Those very Russian citizens were almost exclusively Jewish, hence the expulsion caused a chorus of outrage among the Jewish communities, including those in Europe. Soon Bek was renowned for his rigorous and brutal clampdown. Legend has it that he would arrest people in the street and force them to work for his city development projects. This course of action also led to the relocation of some Muslim cemeteries which is against the religious law. Tel Aviv's Rothschild Boulevard became the model for Jaffa's Jerusalem Boulevard, at that time named "Jamal Pasha Boulevard." Pasha was the governor of Syria since 1915. After two years in office, Bek was removed.

The "Pioneers' House," a Jewish hostel in Yefet Street, also became one of the targets during the excesses of 1921. An Arabic mob had forced their entry into the house and even local police did not stop them. A Jewish policeman who came by accidentally put the aggressors to flight by the use of his gun. At this point, 14 guests were already dead and the others were hiding on the second floor. A few weeks later the hostel moved to Allenby Street. The consistent assaults provoked the British rulers to broaden the streets in Jaffa to make them easier to patrol with military vehicles; about 250 houses were demolished.

In the two-state-solution, a suggestion from the UN published in November 1947, Jaffa was supposed to be an enclave on Jewish territory. But at this time the two parties were already at war with each other and the UN solution did not seem feasible any longer. The Brits decide to leave Palestine. In November 1947 the first mass exodus set in. About 30,000 Arabs left Jaffa, mainly for Gaza and Beirut. The conflict between Jews and Arabs became even more heated. In January 1948 the Jewish resistance bombed the Saray building, the seat of the Arab administration and End of April the "Irgun" (also called "Etzel") took over Manshiye. In the days following this event the fighters of the Hagana movement conquered the villages outside Jaffa. The British military showed a massive presence in Jaffa but the last 70,000 citizens decided to leave. On 13 May 1948 Jaffa surrendered and the remaining 3,000 people of the former metropolitan city gathered in Ajami. After the founding of the State of Israel on 14 May 1948 the Jews were expelled from the neighboring Arab countries; another mass exodus set in, this time to Jaffa, where only weeks before the Arab population had casted off. They arrived in a deserted town and settled wherever they found a place.

In the 1950s the new developments started in Jaffa and not very much was preserved. Since 1950 Tel Aviv and Jaffa are united and the city's official name is Tel Aviv-Yafo. The many immigrants changed the face of the city and new houses mushroomed everywhere. In the original plans high-rise buildings were supposed to give room to the new citizens; nobody seemed to be interested in preserving anything from the past. Manshiye was completely erased from the landscape in 1963 when the last ruins were demolished. When the harbor of Ashkelon opened in 1965, the golden times of the Jaffa port were finally over and the area became desolate. It was a group of artists who would convince then-mayor Shlomo Lahat in the 1970s to preserve Jaffa. Until today Jaffa is affected by social conflicts, especially because of rising prices for housing. The recent renovations and new construction attract a wealthier and Jewish audience and the local population feels threatened. This forms an excellent breeding ground for Islamic groups. Since 1999 the municipality is investing in the revitalization of Jaffa, a term that does not mean the same to all involved. Today, not much remains of the former Jaffa. The authentic Jaffa can still be found, but only in the hidden little streets, off the beaten tourist path.

Jaffa remains a sore point in the Mideast conflict. Jaffa was the pride of the Arabic population. Why was it abandoned? The reasons are manifold; one is that the Jews had been fed up since the consistent assaults in 1921 and the Arab population feared revenge. The British police had their own daily fight with the Jewish resistance groups and nobody had any confidence in them protecting Jaffa and its population. The Jewish elite had prepared their independence for decades while the Arabs were without a leader and organizational structure. It had been a catastrophe – nakba – to abandon Jaffa. The "Bride of the Sea" as they called the city, had been the political and cultural cradle of the population. Intellectuals and rich merchants had lived here, where the most important newspapers of Palestine were once published. Feelings of anger, impotence and humiliation come up again when they think of Jaffa.

3.2 Tel Aviv

The oldest and still visible part of Tel Aviv is not Neve Tzedek, it is the Templer settlement "Sarona", locally known as HaKirya ("the campus.") After the founding of the State of Israel in May 1948 this area served as the first government seat of the young state. Another settlement – Mount Hope, founded in 1849 – is unfortunately not visible anymore. It was located close to today's motorway junction LaGuardia Interchange in the south of Tel Aviv on the campus of the Shva Mofet High School (HaMasger Street.) The city development has also been significantly influenced by every Aliya, the Jewish immigration to Israel. On 11 April 1909 the newly acquired plots of land, sand dunes, were split among the new owners and the construction of the first houses began. The motivation for this very project can be best understood in the historical context.

Mount Hope (1849–1853)

In the middle of the 19th century many Christians in the US and Europe were convinced that the Messiah would come back soon. A group of German and American Christians, among them the John Steinbeck's German grandparents, came into the country and together they founded the settlement of Mount Hope in 1849. Their mission consisted of teaching the local Jews agriculture and Christianity. Moses Montefiori, a British-Jewish philanthropist, visited the Holy Land to buy plots of land and finally purchased the Mount Hope orchid plantations from Rabbi Yehuda HaLevi. The area is still called the Montefiori quarter. On the night of 11 January 1858, the Christian settlers were attacked by a group of Arabs without any previous incident or warning. The village was looted, some men were murdered and their wives raped. The reasons for this brutal assault have never been identified. Interviewed by the Police, the settlers would say that they believe that their successful farming had been the subject of envy among the Arab neighbors. Nevertheless, only a few months later, they would abandon their mission in the Holy

Land and move together to the USA.

The German Templers (1869-1949)

When Tel Aviv started looking into its own young history, the Templers would surface again. They were the group that had most significantly influenced the development of the country and served as a model for the founders of Tel Aviv. They had the most modern houses, applied the latest technology in all their activities and managed to live absolutely independently in the Holy Land. They did not see their mission in teaching Christianity to Jews or Muslims, rather being a living example by living an exemplary life, preferably in the Holy Land, the home of Jesus Christ. This is how they had defined their goal when they split from the National Church in 1861. Christoph Hofmann (1815-1885) and his followers founded their own church – The Temple Society – in Kirschenhardthof, a village 40 km north-east of Stuttgart in Southern Germany (Baden-Württemberg.) The Templers are often mistaken for the Knights Templar, a Christian military order that was active in the 12th century and responsible for the Crusades, but they have nothing more in common than the name.

In 1867 a small group from Germany did not want to wait any longer and decided to move to the Holy Land, without any support from the other Templers. They settled in the Jezreel Valley in the north of the country, between the Galilee and Samaria – a fatal decision. In this sparsely populated area most of them would die in the following years, mainly from malaria. After this tragedy the Temple Society planned very carefully and strategically to where to move. The following settlements were finally realized:

Haifa: 1869

Jaffa: 1869 (purchase of the American settlement)

Sarona: 1871 (purchase of 60 hectares of non-arable land from Arabic owner)

Neuhardthof: 1888 (extension of Haifa)

Walhalla: 1888 (extension of Jaffa)

Rephaim: 1873 (close to Jerusalem)

Wilhelma: 1902 (today Bnei Atarot)

Bethlehem: 1906

After the purchase of the American settlement in 1869, the Templers bought the plots that were later known as Sarona, east of Jaffa. Today Kaplan Street crosses the former Sarona and connects Dizengoff Square with the Azrieli Center and its surrounding business district. At the end of the 19th century people from all over would immigrate to Palestine; Muslims, Jews, Christians, but none of these groups invested so much of their energy and knowledge into the future of this geographical area. The Templers stood out. The hygienic situation of Palestine was a challenge for everybody, but especially for the new immigrants, illnesses like malaria made it even worse. The Sarona plots were especially difficult to cultivate and many were sick. The Templers decided to import eucalyptus trees to drain the swamps. The layout of Sarona was planned strategically: the purchased plots were divided into lots, the new owners determined by lottery. Everybody had enough space to build a home with a little garden. The construction was subject to previously determined rules. Interestingly enough, this was not the last "creative urban planning"; the founders of Tel Aviv would do exactly the same in April 1909: subdivide the plots, establish rules for construction and determine the owners by lottery. The founders of Tel Aviv had studied the Templers very closely, especially their buildings were considered all-time modern. Everywhere in the country where the Templers were active, the general living conditions improved in a short time for everybody living in that area. This was the main motivation for Arabs from other areas to move here. From the Templers they learned efficient agriculture or found work on their plantations. The Templers were completely independent. They cultivated their own oranges, fruits, wine, had cattle breeding and dairies. Among the Templers all kind of professions could be found and their specialists and skilled workers were very popular and busy outside the Templer Society.

During the economic boom Jaffa started expanding outside the original city walls and also the Templers kept an eye out for new plots. They found a well located area right on the border between Neve Tzedek and Jaffa near where the train was supposed to run in the near future. Here they built their industry (e.g. the water pump factory of Wilhelm and Georg Wagner) and some housing.

The Templers were proud Germans but they considered Palestine "home." None of them had ever thought of going back to Germany; they had invested so much energy and money here, giving up was simply not an option. Since they had dissociated themselves from the German National Church they did not get financial help from anybody, unlike other Christian missions. The reclaiming of the plots and the life they had built was their very own success and they felt like they were a part of the country. Until the end of 1917 Palestine was ruled by the Ottomans. The Turks were quite suspicious of foreigners and other religions but the Templers refused the Ottomans' offer to exchange their German passports for Turkish ones even though this could have gained them many advantages in daily life, especially when permits were needed. On the other hand the Ottomans recognized the Templers' expertise in many areas like the British later did. Several bridges and train stations in Palestine were built by the Templers' engineer Josef Wennagel.

At the end of World War I the British had defeated the Ottomans and life would dramatically change for the Templers, gradually leading to the end of their existence in Palestine. The British accused them of spying for Germany and Turkey and decided to deport them. Most of them would spend the following two years in Helouan, close to Cairo, Egypt. Back in Palestine they would find their settlements in deplorable state. Their houses were looted, the factories and plantations neglected. Nevertheless, the Templers rolled up their sleeves and built it up once again.

In the 1920s more and more Jews immigrated to Palestine, some following the Zionist dream, others fleeing the uprising anti-Semitism especially in Eastern Europe. This development would lead to even more resentments among the Arab population who felt seriously threatened by the Jewish salesmanship which resulted in an increasing number of assaults against Jews. The Templers remained neutral. They needed the Arab labor and the Jewish clients, but their German nationalism helped the Nazi party (NSDAP) undermine the community. The keeping of German traditions was the perfect stepping stone for the introduction of Nazi ideology which caused tensions among the Templers. Not every Templer was by definition pro-Nazi only because he worshipped in German and wanted to keep national traditions alive. Many saw a contradiction between Nazi ideology and Christian teaching. But most of them did believe that a strong Germany would be helpful for Germans living abroad. In this context it is no surprise that there would later be groups of the Hitler Youth (Hitlerjugend) in Jaffa, a shock for those Jews who had barely escaped Nazi Germany and hardly made it to Palestine because of the British immigration quota that was intended to appease the Arab population and keep all options open in the Middle East where oil had been found. Sarona was located outside Jaffa and most of the time the Templers would take a moped or a bike to Jaffa. How could they show the Arab snipers that they were not Jews? The Nazi flag with the swastika was well understood.

With the beginning of World War II and the involvement of the United Kingdom it was time to act on the British Mandate of Palestine. The Templers were only good for one reason: they supplied the British with good food including excellent wine, but they were Germans and Germany was the enemy. It was simply unacceptable having the enemy in their own territory. At the same time the overall situation in Palestine became ungovernable: the Jews were hostile against the German Templers because of their affinity with the Nazis, the Arabs attacked the Jews – and often also the British as an expression of their disappointment that their collaboration against the Ottomans had not brought them the promised independence. The British decided to start with the Templers though they had no idea to where to deport them; most of them were born in Palestine.

The Wagner family belonged to those Templers who had already been pro-Arab in 1921 during the Arab assaults. Later they would openly sympathize with the Nazis. Even though they had also been interned in an enemy aliens' camp, the British allowed them to re-open their factories after 1945. The Jews were outraged; after the war the atrocities of the Nazis were known all over the world. In March 1946, Gotthilf Wagner was murdered on Levanda Street. The authorities suspected a Jewish resistance group behind this unsolved murder case.

In the following years the deportees were shipped from one camp to another and back to Sarona, only few deciding to move to Germany. In 1948 they are finally transported to Famagusta, Cyprus, and later, in 1948, to Australia.

First Aliya (1882–1903)
The first Aliya of the Zionist would ultimately overwhelm Jaffa. Haifa and Jaffa were the only harbors at the shallow coastline and therefore, the first arrival place of all immigrants from which many of them would not want to move on. The ancient city with its narrow little streets was soon about to collapse. The housing shortage was severe and hygiene practically absent; the lack of a sewage system would make things even worse. Living in Jaffa would soon turn into a realistic threat to one's health. The European Jews in particular could not see themselves adapt to this kind of life. A group of wealthy Sephardic Jews decided to build a new settlement outside Jaffa and bought plots of land. In 1887, the first Jewish settlement outside Jaffa was founded: Neve Tzedek (Hebrew for "Oasis of Justice") and in 1890, Neve Shalom (Hebrew for "Oasis of Peace") would follow. The latter was built right next to Neve Tzedek for the less wealthy.

Herzl and the dream of "The Jewish State" (1896–1904)
Theodor Herzl (1860–1904), in Israel Binyamin Herzl was an Austro-Hungarian writer and journalist and is considered the founder of international Zionism. When his book "The Jewish State" (in German "Der Judenstaat") was published in February 1896, in Vienna, nobody could have even dreamed that this was the blueprint of the Jewish State to come and not only an essay on Zionism. Herzl's description of the Jews' misery, the necessity for their own state and his vision on the future political development is so much beyond belief as is the timeliness that is impressed on today's reader. Herzl draws a blueprint on how to establish a Jewish

state and most of it was realized in the exact same way, here in Tel Aviv. It was the first Jewish city, founded by Jews and constructed by Jews for Jews. It was the first capital of Israel and a test field for everything to come. Nearly all institutions that were founded with the aim of the establishment of a Jewish state were located in Tel Aviv. Here the corner stones were laid for a new Jewish society; a free society, independent from non-Jews and self-determined, not reduced to its religion but recognizing the religious values as its pillars. Many of the European Jews were not very religious but the society they lived in and for which they had fought in wars did not integrate them; they were simply Jews. Herzl described it in the following way:

Attacks in Parliaments, in assemblies, in the press, in the pulpit, in the street, on journeys--for example, their exclusion from certain hotels--even in places of recreation, become more numerous daily. The forms of persecution vary according to the countries and social circles in which they occur. In Russia, imposts are levied on Jewish villages; in Romania, a few persons are put to death; in Germany, they get a good beating occasionally; in Austria, Anti-Semites exercise terrorism over all public life; in Algeria, there are traveling agitators; in Paris, the Jews are shut out of the so-called best social circles and excluded from clubs. Shades of anti-Jewish feeling are innumerable.

The book provoked very different reactions among Jews and non-Jews but what annoyed Herzl most was that it would be classified as utopia. His book picks up the "Jewish Question" that – according to Herzl – has not been given a solution since the Middle Ages. At the end of every Pessah celebration Jews say "Next year in Jerusalem!" Since the destruction of the Second Temple in the year 70 CE and the Romans coming into power, the Jews have been dreaming of coming back to their country and to found the State of Israel in the Land of Israel. Even in times of uncertainty and prosecution the Jews always hesitated to leave the country they were living in; they simply did not know where to go and this would not change if they did not have their own State. Herzl drew a concrete and detailed roadmap that was based on two pillars: the Society of Jews and the Jewish Company. He also suggested several ways to finance this project.

The task of the Society of Jews was primarily to build the nation and to prepare the political and economic conditions while the Jewish Company should take care of their execution. Palestine was chosen as this future home due to the historic Jewish ties to this piece of land. According to Herzl the land was the only resource that required approval from outside the community. He was confident that those countries with strong anti-Semitism would happily support a Jewish state. He knew that the country was mostly not arable. He suggests that the poorest of the poor immigrate first. They had never lost their belief in the Holy Land and nothing tied them to their country of residence except misery. Russia and Romania seemed to be ideal for the first recruitment.

The main tasks of the Jewish Company were the acquisition of land under private law that later should be guaranteed under international law. The workers would construct their shared residences for each other; simple and functional accommodation. The apartment block in Frishman Street 33-35 is an example of those days. Those workers were supposed to build up the whole country, starting with the residence and continuing with the infrastructure. An incoming agency would filter the stream of immigrants and they would settle next to their work. The remaining Jewish assets that could not be taken to Palestine would be listed for potential sale to Christians.

At the end of August 1897, Herzl held the World Congress of Zionism in Basle where the Basle Program was agreed: "Zionism seeks the creation of a secure home for the Jewish people under public law." On 3 September 1897, Herzl wrote into his diary: "If I summarize the congress of Basle in one word – which I will be wary of saying out loud in public – it will be this: in Basle I founded the Jewish State. If I said that in public I would face a broad laughter. Maybe in 5 years, but definitely in 50 years, they will all agree."

Second Aliya (1904–1914)

This is one of the most important periods in regard to the founding of Tel Aviv. It is the time when the founding fathers immigrate. Still today the historians are wondering if "Achuzat Beit" as Tel Aviv was called at the beginning, was meant to be only a suburb with little nice gardens or whether this was only the embryo of the already imagined Jewish metropolis à la Herzl, a Jewish city for a Jewish state. We will never know. But it is a fact that Tel Aviv was not founded to leave Jaffa, this is what Neve Tzedek and Neve Shalom were for. The immigrating Europeans from places like Odessa, Kiev, Berlin and Budapest could simply not adapt to the Oriental way of life. In 1904, the Kerem HaTeimanim (vineyard of the Yemenites) neighborhood was founded by immigrants from Yemen. They were Zionists, too, but not in a political way and their lifestyle was more in tune with the oriental culture.

Under the auspices of Akiva Aryé Weiss the building society "Achuzat Beit" was founded in 1906 with the main purpose of building this new suburb of which the Europeans had been dreaming. The current Jewish suburbs were too oriental to fuel immigration from Europe: still no sewage system, the streets were dirty and most public spaces neglected. The settlement of the Templer Society, Sarona, was a model the founders studied meticulously. Sarona was the embodiment of modernity and it had a European look and feel. It was no wonder that on 11 April 1909, the distribution of the lots of land to the first 66 families had been organized the Templers' way. The rules for the new owners were similar. They were allowed to build as they liked on their own piece of land with only few restriction, e.g. only one third of the space could be built on. For the public spaces, it was necessary to appoint an architect. Like the Templers, the Ashkenazim had little relation with the sea and started to flatten the sand dunes with their back to the water. The first building was finished in October 1909, and in 1910 the suburb was renamed "Tel Aviv", the title Nachum Sokolow had given the Hebrew translation of Herzl's book "Altneuland."

The most prominent founding fathers were Meir Dizengoff (1861-1936, originally from Moldavia) and Akiva Aryé Weiss (1868-1947 from Belarus.) Dizengoff came to Jaffa in 1905. The charismatic and handsome business man soon gained influence in Jewish society. He invested in many different fields and would soon start buying plots of land outside Jaffa. Weiss arrived in Jaffa in 1906 coming from ?ód?, Poland. He was determined to execute Herzl's plan; a Jewish society needed a Jewish city. In his opinion the agricultural settlements and the embellishment of existing buildings was simply not enough. He envisioned a large Tel Aviv for a new society. The day of his arrival he went to the first local meeting. The popular demand of his ideas resulted in his assignment for the execution. The building society "Achuzat Beit" was founded and soon construction of the first buildings started. When "Achuzat Beit" was finished in 1910, Weiss could not find any supporters for his plans for expansion and he decided to leave and invest in his own projects. Weiss contributed significantly to the development of the country by founding several factories and companies, like the "Ora Hadasha" movie company. He was also the builder of the "Eden Cinema" and the first post office building of the city. Later he would initiate the "Diamond Club", the embryo of today's Diamond Exchange.

Dizengoff had been cooperating right from the beginning with the "Achuzat Beit" society for the purchase of land. In 1911 he became chief city planner and 1922, the city's first mayor. During the following years Dizengoff practically eliminated Weiss from history and promoted himself as the initiator of the city who had smartly led the development from suburb to metropolis. The fact that the first plans for expansions had come from Weiss was omitted as were the main contributions of the Scottish city planner Patrick Geddes.

The British government published the Balfour Declaration on 2 November 1917, shortly after General Allenby had conquered the city of Beer Sheva and ended the Ottoman reign. In the Balfour Declaration the British committed themselves to help the Jews get a national home. During the British Mandate, Jews were allowed to immigrate to Palestine but there was no support available in any other aspect.

Third Aliya (1919–1923)

The 1st of May of 1921 was the day Jews would not forget for a long time. It was the day of Arab assaults on Jewish demonstrators. Two Jewish groups violently clashed during Labor Day demonstrations. The demonstration of the Jewish Communist Party had been authorized, but the Workers' Union (today Israel's Workers' Party, then lead by David Ben-Gurion) had called for an unauthorized countermarch. Both groups were knocking each other around when suddenly an Arab group gathered to beat up the Jews, the violence escalated and lead to shootings and more violence. The Arab Police ignored the incident. The Jews were in shock. The civil population organized themselves and sealed off Tel Aviv. In the days that followed they picked up the remaining Jews in Jaffa and cast out Arabs from Jewish neighborhoods. At the end Jaffa was purely Arabic, an apparent victory for the aggressors that would soon backfire. The "assaults of Jaffa" went on for three days, but in this first week of May, Jews were attacked by Arabs all over the country. Life would change forever.

After the assault, the British High Commissioner Lord Herbert Samuel soon reorganized the administration: in June 1921, Tel Aviv was granted some autonomy and could impose tax. Until 1923, it was still mandated by Jaffa, later it was gathered with Neve Tzedek, Neve Shalom and Kerem HaTeimanim as well as all the purchased plots. Jaffa, the economic center until then, got cut off and suddenly there was a real gap between clients and merchants. For the latter, it was much more difficult to swallow. The Jews would avoid Jaffa. The new municipality stressed on the expansion towards the Yarkon River in the north – without Arab labor – and opened new shops; the products were imported from Europe and the money, too. Jaffa sank into poverty. The port business "saved" Jaffa until 1933. This was the year when the Haifa port opened and the monopoly fell. The border between Jaffa and Tel Aviv was drawn on Daniel Street, south of the Yemenite Quarter, on the other side of Manshiye. This area was the scene of fights between Arabs and Jews

47

since then, especially in the 1940s.

The development of Tel Aviv benefitted from the events that reminded many citizens of Herzl. Self-supply and the responsibility for the own safety were the immediate tasks to fulfill. All labor became exclusively Jewish and the clichés would disappear. Being able to plan the future had been a Jewish dream for too long and now, for the first time, they had the chance to take care of their own destiny. The new immigrants of the third Aliya had to live in tents on the plots in the north. The Palestine Land Development Company would from now on be in charge of the purchase of new land.

Fourth Aliya (1924-1929)

These were the golden days of Tel Aviv. The cultural life was booming and well educated Europeans immigrated. The municipality appointed the Scotsman Patrick Geddes as strategic city planner, a so far unknown profession. Patrick gave the development the necessary rebound. Until now, all the planning only considered those plots of land that had already been purchased. Geddes would freely draw a new map, disregarding land ownership. He concentrated on large north-south and east-west connections. Geddes was a biologist. He studied closely the relationship between beings, in this case: the citizens. Where did they go, on which ways, who met who? He identified big streets for the main traffic, the access to the houses where wives and mothers interacted were already significantly smaller. The ways to the bakery as well as to the parks were supposed to be short. Here, where mothers and children lived, main traffic should be avoided. Geddes was not Jewish but sympathized with Zionism. Although Tel Aviv was a secular city, they all wanted to live in a society based on Jewish values. They agreed that Jewish holidays would be days off and celebrated in public. A synagogue was not the center of daily life anymore but still a main part of the culture and, therefore, should be in reasonable reach. Geddes understood the task. He took all those elements together to lead Judaism from religion to culture. Theaters, libraries and boulevards were the new center of public life. He also examined the local climate and the challenges it presented. He was the first in planning cubic houses with roof terraces, not those architects who would later earn their diplomas in Europe. Geddes understood the Jews' search for a new, modern Jewish society and avoiding any impression of tightness. In his planning, he left out a considerable amount of space for green areas. The city was supposed to be light and the buildings should not remind of the European "Shtetls", away from walls and cemeteries. In 1925 he presented a plan in which he planned the city from Bograshov Street up to the Yarkon River, the eastern border was Ibn Gvirol Street.

From 1927, it became increasingly difficult to get a building permit from the

48

authorities in Jerusalem because High Commissioner Lord Herbert Samuel had been replaced by Lord Plumer. More and more, the Brits would reduce Tel Aviv's newly gained autonomy, especially their finances. From now on, the city expansion had to rely on donations only instead of taxes. At the same time, land to buy was getting scarce and the municipality would pass a new bill that allowed the expropriation of land from owners to win space which was more needed than ever from 1933 onwards.

Fifth Aliya (1929-1939)

Tel Aviv was finally running out of space and at the same time new immigrants would flood the country. The British bureaucracy for building permits would slow down construction activities, the rest of the world was suffering from an economic crisis and not much money was sent to support the projects in Tel Aviv. It had turned into a vibrant, European-style city; most of the new European immigrants did not want to move on to other parts of the country and stayed in Tel Aviv. As a result, it had become impossible to keep all the green areas that Geddes had planned. Even existing gardens and parks had to give way. According to reports from that time, between 1931 and 1935, the population had tripled and reached 120,000. In 1934, the Jewish National Fund was able to purchase new plots of land in the north. Hence, mainly immigrants from Germany and Hungary, where the majority of immigrants came from, would settle in this area. Though all the labor was Jewish, the unemployment rate was very high. The Jewish society would drift apart into European Jews (Ashkenazim) and Oriental Jews (Sephardim.) The Ashkenazim would live in the north, the Sephardim in the south. This has not changed through today, only the distribution of unemployment is different: today, there are more people in the south without a job. The new immigrants at that time would all go north. The German Jews had the most difficulties in adapting. Most of them had been very established with a "normal" life in Germany until the Nazis came to power, so adapting to their new home proved difficult, unlike the Eastern European Jews who had integrated well in the new land and picked up the language very fast. For the "Jeckes" (pronounced: yeckes), as the Germans were called – because they always kept their jacket on, even in the summer heat, and hardly spoke Hebrew – the Eastern Europeans had no respect.

1936 was an emotional year for Tel Aviv and Israel in general. It was the year when the Arabic Revolt started that would not stop until 1939. Their leader was the Grand Mufti of Jerusalem, Mohammed Amin al-Husseini, who was on friendly terms with Nazi Germany and had significantly introduced the idea of anti-Semitism in the Arab world. In Syria and Egypt, the Arab workers had already been successful with their work stoppage and negotiations on their independence from France, and the British Crown had already been on their way.

On 17 May 1936, the works for the new Tel Aviv port started. This was another step towards independence; there was no other harbor between Haifa and Jaffa. The coast is very shallow here and big ships came as close as they could, then the passengers as well as the goods had to be transshipped into small rowing boats. This business was nearly 100% Arabic. Since the assaults from 1921, confidence in the Arab neighbors had vanished and nobody could still imagine a peaceful co-existence. These worries were fueled by the massacres from Hebron and Safed in 1929, and the attacks would not stop in the years to come. The landing in the port of Jaffa would take longer with every ship that entered due to increasing immigration and the expansion of the local economy. Oftentimes, the ships would have to wait for several days for their unloading. On 13 December 1934, two ships collided with each other close to the Yarkon estuary in the north, hence, a lighthouse was built in January 1935, close to today's port. A new port was the only solution. The name of the street closest to the port refers to those days: "She's Zion Street", the gate of Zion. In 1949, the municipality started an expansion of the Tel Aviv harbor by deepening it. This way, ships could enter the port and did not have to be unloaded at sea. The Grand Mufti ended the Arab strike in October 1936, and one month later the British would found the Peel Commission to investigate the Arab Revolt.

1936 was also the year the municipality constructed the Ben-Gurion airport between Tel Aviv and Jerusalem that would initially be open only for military usage.

The Peel Commission declared in July 1937 that the strong anti-Semitism among the Muslim population could lead to only one possible solution: the separation into two states. Even though the Jewish part was much smaller and the Arabs had already been granted the whole territory east of the Jordan river (today known as the "Kingdom of Jordan"), the Arabs refused and the Grand Mufti would start the revolt again. At the end of that year, there were mass revolts and assaults on Brits and Jews but this time the attackers came from the rural population. The mayor of Tel Aviv, Israel Roach, asked the British Mandate government for a permit to build an airport for Tel Aviv. Traveling had become a huge risk for Jews. The airport Sadeh Dov was inaugurated in 1938 and offered regular flights to Haifa. The results of the Peel Commission led the British to give major concessions to the Arabs. Most probably, this move was motivated by the Crown's interest in the Middle East and the assumption that the Jews would depend on them. The next steps would be cemented in the "White Paper of 1939": in the following 5 years, only a maximum of 75,000 Jews were allowed to immigrate; any higher number would be subject to Arab approval. At the same, time the purchase of land through Jews became very much restricted.

World War II (1939-1945)

On 9 September 1940, Tel Aviv suffered its first air bombing, and without any prior warning and medical infrastructure in place. It was a hit from Mussolini against the British. The damages were considerable and 137 people lost their lives. Most of the victims were "residents" of the tent settlements that were not even equipped to withstand a major storm. A memorial stone reminds of this incident on the corner of King George Street and Ben Zion Boulevard. Less than a year later, the Vichy regime sent bombs to Tel Aviv; this time 20 people died.

End of the Palestine Mandate (1947-1948)

The British government decided to give up their mandate in 1948. The years of 1948 and 1947 felt like civil war. Jewish resistance fighters and Arab snipers fought each other violently. In December 1947, the Jewish National Fund managed to purchase the Templer compound of Sarona from the Mandate parliament. The municipality had now gained land of an important size. This was not for residential purposes; they were looking for the future government seat of the state they were about to create. The area was renamed HaKirya, the campus, and "Sarona" would not be heard or read for a long time. On 5 Iyar 5708 (14 May 1948), David Ben-Gurion formally proclaimed the establishment of the State of Israel. At the end of the same year, the decision was taken to group Jaffa and Tel Aviv in one city which finally happened in 1950.

Until today, there is a still a north-south division in Tel Aviv, though the municipality is trying to modernize the southern districts, including Jaffa, but the local residents simply cannot keep up with the modernization. Rents are rising and many have to give way to residential luxury projects and live in poverty. The protests on Rothschild Boulevard in 2011 have shown that this problem is not limited to the southern districts only anymore.

3.2.1   Tel Aviv today

Tel Aviv can be roughly divided into 5 districts:

- North
- Northern Center
- Center
- South
- Jaffa

Patrick Geddes had planned the city up to the Yarkon Park, which for a long time was the city's northern border. Today, the **North** stops where Herzliya, the next city, begins. The stylish towers with its condominiums for the wealthier residents as well as the University are located north of the Park. Locals call the part between Ben-Gurion Boulevard and Yarkon Park the "old North", though correctly this would only apply to the area west of Ibn Gvirol Street. Geddes' plan had not included the areas further east. The now closed-down Tel Aviv port is also located in the "old North" and offers night life, bars, restaurants, coffee shops right next to the sea. And last but not least, Dizengoff Street is a very prominent old-time witness with its elegant shops.

The famous Dizengoff Square with its classical International Style architecture is located in the **Northern Center**. Most of the buildings from the 1930s are located here. Between Ben-Gurion Boulevard and Bograshov Street, 75% of the buildings belong to the "White City" as defined by the UNESCO.

Tel Aviv's **center** is rich in history. This is where everything began: the first houses of Achuzat Beit and the Rothschild Boulevard were located here, as well as the first Jewish high school. Later, in 1948, the State of Israel was formally proclaimed on Rothschild Boulevard No. 16. The center is also called "Lev HaIr" – heart of the city. The streets already existed in old plans from 1924, but some of the houses were constructed later.

The districts of Neve Tzedek and Florentin form the **South**. Shortly before the end of the century, Jaffa had started to expand. The Maronite Christians would found Ajami in the south of Jaffa, the Muslims went north and settled where today the Charles Clore Park can be found and the Jews founded Neve Tzedek. Some 30 years later, Florentin was founded by Greek Jews from Saloniki. The cornerstone for the Kerem HaTeimanim was laid in 1904 but because of its geographic location, it is not part of the South. Jaffa is also south, but it is mostly mentioned apart.

Jaffa, "the beauty", with its medieval history and the exceptional fusion of Arabic and European culture, different religions, architecture and ethno food extends to Bat Yam, the next city in the south.

4 Architecture

When Tel Aviv was founded in 1909 as Achuzat Beit, the modern architecture had not yet been invented. The construction left and right of Rothschild Boulevard combined all different kinds of styles. This sometimes "wild" style combination is called Eclectic Style. The owners had in mind the houses from the countries they have left behind, adapted this mostly Middle- and Eastern-European style to the trends of that time and the oriental elements they found at site. The pointed windows in the Ottoman style were especially very popular. European architects had come to visit Palestine long before the 1930s. They did not come to check out Aliya possibilities, they were simply attracted by the opportunities this empty piece of land would offer to architects. Tel Aviv was a test field in many areas. City development, as it is known today, did not exist back then. The unrestricted planning of a completely new town was a great chance that would not come back soon. In the 1920s, Tel Aviv blossomed, its cultural scene being as abundant as that in Berlin or Budapest. The city kept growing and new construction surfaced everywhere: movie and stage theaters were built and Europe's intellectuals could not resist the city's charm. The cultural life was booming. The purchased land was rapidly covered with buildings and each time the houses would look more modern. The years of heavy immigration, especially at the end of the 1920 and again after 1948, posed the challenge to rapidly construct cheap residential buildings. Under this pressure, more than one historic building was sacrificed.

When Tel Aviv was awarded the UNESCO World Heritage status on 3 July 2003, nobody would have even dreamed that this would be tourism magnet of the near future. Even new construction is designed in the International Style again. "Bauhaus" is a term that seems to be intrinsically tied to Tel Aviv. Does this mean that every International Style building is a "Bauhaus"? The document from the UNESCO refers to the "White City of Tel Aviv – The Modern Movement." Tel Aviv is home to over 4,000 buildings from the 1930s, many in deplorable state. What exactly was "The Modern Movement" in architecture? Different but similar ideas can be identified, but no exact criteria for a definite and clear classification. Some examples:

- New Building (from German: Neues Bauen)
- Bauhaus
- New Objectivity (from German: Neue Sachlichkeit)
- International Style

New Building

This totally new way of building would be applied mainly between 1910 and the 1930s. The architects would use different, new material – like glass, steel, iron – and pre-fabricated construction elements to create more spacious and especially lighter rooms. This was understood as a counterbalance to the predominant mainly shady backyards and the tenement houses. Building was being streamlined.

Bauhaus

In 1919, Walter Gropius founded the Bauhaus school (in German "Staatliches Bauhaus") in Dessau. The principle idea was to unite crafts and the manual arts to create something new that would combine art and production with the final goal to eliminate the society's hierarchies, called classes. The artist was for Gropius the epitome of the craftsman. The artisan tradition was the base of creation that was finally supposed to lead to a more humane society. During the first Bauhaus exhibition in 1923, the proto-type of Bauhaus architecture was presented. In only 4 months, the building "Haus am Horn" (German: house at the horn), designed by Georg Muche, was constructed in Weimar. It was meant to be a livable prototype and first representative of a future settlement for the Bauhaus professors. The whole settlement was actually realized later in Dessau. The building disposed of a simple cube with a functional and sober interior architecture. This was very typical for the beginnings of the involvement of the Bauhaus school in architecture. The Haus am Horn was seen as a representative of the New Building. Already in 1922, Gropius had presented a nowadays renowned sketch for the new construction of the "Chicago Tribune" skyscraper. This "classical Bauhaus building", is characterized with its clear lines and much glass. Unfortunately it was never realized. The one element that can be found in all Bauhaus buildings is the usage of pre-fabricated building parts that can be individually adapted to its final purpose. Building according to the Bauhaus school meant to use a "kit", like combs – as Gropius would say.

The members of the Bauhaus school were considered leftwing and because of their socialistic ideas, they were a thorn in the Nazis' side. After the Nazis won the elections, the Bauhaus school – now in Berlin because in Dessau they were closed already – was forced to close in July 1933. Many of the members emigrated and continued their work in their new country, mostly in the USA. This is how the Bauhaus principles got introduced on the other side of the ocean.

New Objectivity

The term applies to those buildings that were later built in the "Bauhaus Style" but not by a member from the Bauhaus school.

International Style

The architectural historian Henry-Russell Hitchcock (1903-1987) and the architect Philip Johnson (1906-2005) used this term to describe the minimalistic and functional elements of the architecture in the 1920s and 1930s. In Tel Aviv, there are about 4,000 buildings that belong into this category.

4.1 The Influence of Le Corbusier

Le Corbusier (1887-1965) was Ze'ev Rechter's mentor and, therefore, it is not a surprise that the latter would be the first to build a house on pillars (Engel House, 84, Rothschild Blvd.) because this was just his mentor's very own signature. In the 1920s, Le Corbusier developed "The Five Points of Architecture": pillars (pilotis), roof garden, free façade (non supporting walls), free floor plan and long strips of ribbon windows. The pillars guaranteed the green area and the roof garden created even more. With the support of the pillars, there was no need anymore for supporting walls and all static requirements were abolished and the floor planning became totally free. Consequently, the facades could be opened anywhere and windows did not have to be installed upright anymore, they could also be crosswise.

All five elements can be indentified in Tel Aviv within the White City. Together with Max du Bois, Le Corbusier owned a patent for the building of prefabricated houses with steel frame. Tel Aviv's fast development and expansion has benefited abundantly from Le Corbusier's inventions. For him, economical and functional construction was the logical answer to the technical progress in the world, that which would result in fast-happening changes in people's environment and lifestyle.

4.2 The White City

The White City encompasses mainly the area south of Ben-Gurion Boulevard, west of Rothschild and Chen Boulevard. The vast majority of the buildings here represent the New Objectivity and the International Style respectively, though Israelis love to present every building as a "Bauhaus." The principles of the Bauhaus school have been applied in many buildings at least partially, e.g. with the roof garden for all tenants, or the workers' residence in Frishman Street 33 where there are big common areas for eating and showing, but no usual flats. Speedy and economical construction became top priority at the latest by the 1930s when the number of immigrants increased. The prefabricated construction elements were ideal. The Bauhaus school has worked a lot with glass and iron to let light and air into the flat but in Tel Aviv, the local climate presented its very own challenges. Light was appreciated but sun was not, the building was not supposed to open towards the south and big windows were avoided. Typical for houses in Tel Aviv are the narrow strips of windows. There was no iron production in Palestine and the use of these pricy imported elements was reduced to a minimum. Unless, it was a private building and the owner was ready to pay for it. Le Corbusier's pillar concept can be found in many buildings, too. It was a great space-saving way to create a little garden when there was actually no space at all for the kind of front garden Patrick Geddes had suggested in his master plan from 1925. Many of the local buildings show a combination of the rectilinear Bauhaus Style and geometric forms. The architects in Tel Aviv used the term "organic architecture". Europeans would have never named it this way since organic architecture for them was just another name for chaos. In Judaism, perfect health is a gift from the creator, hence, also the body and its form. The basic forms – round or edged – create this asymmetry. The masters at the Bauhaus school did not use them in their plans and for this reason, these buildings are clearly of International Style.

"Israeli Box Style"
In the late 1940s, during the struggle for independence, the International Style was minimalized once again. The result was the box. Construction had to be fast, there were no capacities left for any kind of design. This would not change until the mid-1950s. At this time in Israel, more immigrants than ever poured into country. After the state founding, Israel had to take care of itself and at the same time secure its borders. Also, the box buildings were mostly constructed on pillars, but any other style element that locally is called "typically Bauhaus", disappeared.

Exhibition: Batim MiBifnim
Since 2007, Tel Aviv has been a member of the "Open House Family", an organization that organizes visits and guided tours in different cities around the globe. Parks, private houses, public buildings and factories open their doors for one weekend. In Tel Aviv, this free Batim MiBifnim festival (Hebrew for "houses from inside") takes place every year in May. Many walks and guided tours are also held in English. http://www.batim-il.org

4.3   Architects in Tel Aviv

Legend has it that Tel Aviv has been built up by German Jewish architects or prosecuted members of the German Bauhaus movement who came to Palestine to realize their ideas. The truth is that the famous architects were nearly all from Eastern Europe, had made Aliya to Palestine and later went to Europe to study from the local masters. Back in Palestine, they had then constructed in this new architecture language that was not a unique invention from Germany only, but one that was adapted to the local challenges and requirements: climate, socialistic ideas and time pressure to build up the country.

Arieh Sharon (Poland 1900, Israel 1984)

Born Ludwig Kurzmann, Sharon came to Israel in 1920. He was a co-founder of the kibbutz Gan Shmuel and in 1928, he decided to study at the Bauhaus in Dessau, Germany. A year later, he got married to Gunta Stölzl, the Bauhaus master of the weaving mill. His style is minimal as can be seen in the workers' residence Meonot Ovdim that is actually an "urban kibbutz" since it has the same structure for the community spaces (laundry, kitchen, mensa, kindergarten, etc.) The residence in Frishman Street 33-35 is the best known of his urban works. Sharon developed the blue print for the building up of Israel and was the right hand of David Ben-Gurion. He is considered the father of Israeli architecture.

Dov Karmi (Ukraine 1905, Israel 1962)

After immigrating to Israel in 1921, he enrolled some years later at the École des Beaux-Arts in Gent, Belgium. During his most active time from 1930 to 1950, he created more than 50 buildings in the International Style, mainly in Tel Aviv and Jerusalem. Together with Ze'ev Rechter, he won the competition for the Mann Auditorium.

Ze'ev Rechter (Ukraine 1899, Israel 1960)

He made Aliya in 1919 but would later leave the country several times for a longer period to study engineering in Rome and architecture in Paris where he met Le Corbusier. Strongly influenced by Le Corbusier's style, he came back to Tel Aviv and built the Engel House (84, Rothschild Boulevard), the first building on pillars.

Josef Neufeld (Poland 1898, USA 1980)

When he immigrated to the Holy Land in 1920, he had no idea yet that he would become one of the most sought-after international architects of his time. He learned from Erich Mendelsohn in Berlin during the 1920s, came back to Israel, and would finally immigrate to the USA but visited Israel frequently to supervise his projects there.

Genia Averbuch (Russia 1909, Israel 1977)

Her parents made Aliya when she was 2 years old. She studied architecture at several European universities and opened her own office when she came back to Israel in 1930. She won the architecture contest to redesign Dizengoff Square and became the chief city planner of Tel Aviv from 1940-1945.

Richard Kaufmann (Germany 1887, Israel 1958)

He had already opened his own company in 1914 when he met Arthur Ruppin, the director of the Palestine Authority and co-founder of Tel Aviv who finally inspired him to make Aliya in 1920. Long before Patrick Geddes, he had developed a plan for the northern expansion of Tel Aviv. This plan did not find any supporters at that time, but Geddes knew this plan and, it seems, took some ideas out of it to complete his own ideas. Kaufmann had already planned the wide north-south connections disregarding land ownership that can be also found in Geddes' plan.

Josef Berlin (Russia 1900, Israel 1984)

Before he came to Israel in 1921, he had worked in his own business in St. Petersburg. In 1933, his son would join him and together they constructed over 250 buildings until his death in 1984. He was especially renowned for his use of silicate stone.

The Ring – HaChug

In 1926, Sharon, Rechter and Neufeld founded a circle called "HaChug." They were longing for a new architectural language, a new beginning in architecture. Soon they were joined by Rubin, Karmi, Barkai and others. Young architects, especially those with diplomas from Europe, would join them. Together, they wanted to revolutionize the market. The magazine, "HaBinyan BaMisrach Karov" (Hebrew for "Construction in the Middle East,") was another of their activities; the first edition was published in 1934, later changing its name to "HaBinyan" (Hebrew for "The Building.") The magazine was a strong supporter of the current zeitgeist: the search for a new identity through having a Jewish state and a Jewish architectural style. With the increasing problems between the Jewish and Arab populations, the oriental style elements on buildings would soon disappear and architects looked for a "Jewish style."

4.4   UNESCO World Heritage

In 2003, UNESCO awarded Tel Aviv the World Heritage status and recognized the world's biggest coherent ensemble of buildings from the 1930s that were constructed in the International Style. All over Tel Aviv, square-edged houses with round balconies can be found. UNESCO subdivided the city center into zones: A (between Ben-Gurion Boulevard and Bograshov St.), B (around Bialik St.) and C (upper Rothschild Boulevard and Nahmani St., up to the Mann Auditorium.) Together, they form "The White City" with about 4,000 International Style buildings, many still in need of refurbishment today. The municipality made concessions for the refurbishments and allowed the investors to add one or two floors. The original buildings never exceeded three or four floors. The UNESCO-defined zones are home to 2,087 buildings of which 699 are listed.

The following buildings are representative of this era. Most of the buildings are very centrally located, others a bit off the beaten path but worth the walk. Even those buildings that are in a deplorable state still give an idea of the glamour and the spirit of the old times. Stroll through the streets of the White City and breathe the air of nostalgia.

1) 84, Rothschild Boulevard, Engel House (1934), architect: Ze'ev Rechter

The Engel House is a very prominent representative of the "Modern Movement"; it was the first building on pillars in Tel Aviv, a clear style element from Le Corbusier with whom the architect Ze'ev Rechter had worked during his studies in Paris. When the plots became scarce, the pillar construction was the best compromise to construct as much a possible without neglecting the mandatory green area. The roof garden was a symbol of the workers' movement of the 1930s, a space for encounters with the neighbors. The U-shaped floor plan includes a courtyard to the neighboring Mazeh Street.

2) 33-35, Frishman St., workers' residence (1935), architect: Arieh Sharon

Arieh Sharon is considered the father of Israeli architecture. He is also the architect of many kibbutzim and made history as David Ben-Gurion's chief planner to build up Israel. This residence is a very interesting and rare combination of residential building and kibbutz. The workers lived in spartan flats and the mutual activities took place in the basement. As in a kibbutz, there was a mensa and around the courtyard – this building is also u-shaped – the laundry, the kindergarten and the shop for daily supply could be found. Sharon had been a student of the Bauhaus school in Dessau. From his master, the architect Hans Meier, he had adopted the belief that architecture is supposed to improve society.

3) 23, Pinsker St., Mintz & Elenberg House (1935), architect: Philip (Pinchas) Hütt

This house is also known as the "anchor house" in reference to the overall impression of the façade. The staircase is illuminated by the glass elements, a signature of the International Style. The buildings had been originally planned for single women, with 35 little flats.

4) 65, Hovevei Zion St., Mirenberg House (1935), architects: Philip (Pinchas) Hütt

The fusion of two building blocks, as is shown in this construction, is another very typical element of the International Style. Two heavy and independent construction blocks are joined by rounded corners and a shared staircase. The often-found asymmetry is underlined by overhanging wings and integrated balconies.

5) 79, Mazeh St., Recanati House (1935), architects: Shlomo Liaskovski & Yakov Orenstein

The spectacular façade design acts on the idea of "functional asymmetry": a dynamic façade for a dynamic street and a neutral, calm composition for the quiet side street. The figurative element of the repetition of the balconies plays with the natural antithesis of light and shadow. The Bar Orian architecture firm completely refurbished the building in 2000.

6) 22, HaRakevet St., Citrus House (1935), architect: Carl Rubin

The Beit Hadar as it is known in Hebrew shows the influence Mendelsohn had on his student, Carl Rubin. It was the first building with a steel skeleton in Tel Aviv. Three independent, massive constructions seem monstrous and heavy and still, yet they seem to be floating on top of the floor. This illusion is created by the use of the windows on the entire façade on the first floor. Glass was often used to visually mark a separation, here: the shops and the offices.

7) 27, Menachem Begin Road, Gavrilovich House (1936), architects: Y. Kashdan & E. Shimshoni

This building is an example of how freely the architects of the International Style were actually "modeling" their houses. This unusual concept plays with light and shadow, squares and circles as well as with concave and convex. The impression of symmetry and asymmetry is not clear anymore. It seems as if one part of the building was cut out and put back as balconies.

8) Idelson St. 29, Max-Liebling-House (1936), architect: Dov Karmi

When Dov Karmi came back from his studies in Belgium, he would surprise the local market with a new style element: immersed balconies. In summer, they protect from too much sun and heat but in winter, they let light and warmth in. The pillar construction introduced by Ze'ev Rechter allowed building without supporting walls and allowed a free planning of the floor and the façade.

9) Zina Dizengoff Square (1936), architect: Gina Averbuch

The conceptual design of Kikar Zina Dizengoff – as the square is correctly called in Hebrew – is the result of a competition like all the public places and buildings. The winner, Gina Averbuch, offered the best solution for a mutual design for both the square and surrounding buildings. The uniform façade design glamorized the square and gave it a harmonious overall picture. In the original blue print, it was foreseen to elevate the center of the square and to create parking space. This feature was not realized and the square became a roundabout. Decades later, the traffic on Dizengoff Street became a challenge and in 1978, the decision was taken to remodel the square with an underpass. This step diminished a lot the main character of the square. Currently, the municipality is studying the possibility to return to the original blue print. Zina Dizengoff was the mayor's late wife.

10) 14, Ben Ami St./ 8, Beilinson St., Kupat Cholim building (1938), architect: Josef Neufeld

The building that is nowadays home to the Kabbala Center was the first seat of the Kupat Cholim, the public health insurance. The original division was based on a functional subdivision of the building with the laboratories and storage in the basement and the offices on the upper floors. The sunken balconies offer shade and perfect ventilation and in winter; when the sun altitude is much lower, light and warmth still enter the rooms.

11) 1, Zamenhoff St., Esther Cinema (1939), architects: Yehuda & Rafael Magidovitch

The façade design follows exactly the concept suggested by Gina Averbuch for the Dizengoff square. The cinema was built for 1,000 spectators and inaugurated in 1939 with Walt Disney's film, "Snow White and the Seven Dwarfs." It became a reference for cultural life in Tel Aviv. From 1998 to 2000, the building was thoroughly refurbished and later a boutique hotel moved in. The hotel is reminiscent of the cinematic past of this place: the whole place is decorated with exhibits from the former cinema, not only the lobby, but also the rooms.

4.5 New building, old appearance

Tel Aviv's rediscovered identity with the International Style architecture had led to a boom of façade designs in that old style. A growing number of new buildings have been constructed in a design that directly refers to the 1930s. Many times, it is difficult to estimate the period in which a building was constructed. A good example of these new buildings in old appearance is the corner of Tchernichovsky and Dizengoff Street:

12) 69-73, Dizengoff St./ 59, Tchernichovsky St.
In 2001, the architects Ronit and Elisha Rubin built this apartment building with its 23 flats on 4 floors. Like the Recanati House (79, Mazeh Street), this building has two different façade designs with different characters: a dynamic, "loud" one on the side facing Dizengoff Street and a much sober design toward the calm side street Tchenichovsky.

5 Discover Tel Aviv!

In 2009, Tel Aviv celebrated its 100th birthday. Much has happened since then. The city has increasingly opened up for the growing number of tourists. There are many ways to approach the city: through a city tour, a walk on the beach, following the traces of the Templers and Ottomans or in the shade of great architecture.

5.1 Sight-Seeing Tour

The sight-seeing tour gives a good general overview of the city. With a convertible bus, you will see Tel Aviv from north to south in eight languages to choose from. The tour starts in the very north, behind Hangar 4 in the Port of Tel Aviv (exact address: Kaf Gimel Yordey Sira 1). On Friday, the last bus leaves Hangar 4 at 14.00. You can freely hop on and off the bus during the trip; however, the next bus is at least one hour away and might be already full. Here you can see the route: http://www.dan.co.il/download/files/100Nom.pdf

1.) Leaving from Hangar 4: 09.00, 11.00, 12.00, 13.00, 14.00, 15.00, 16.00

5.2 Guided Walks

The municipality offers free walking tours. The tours are held in English, no registration necessary. During the Jewish holidays, there are no tours.

Tel Aviv University: Mondays at 11.00 *
This walk is on the university campus and explains the architecture, the sculptures and the historic background.

2.) Meeting point: Dynanon Bookstore; entrance: Einstein St./ Chaim Levanon St.
* Exception: last week of August.

Tel Aviv by Night: Tuesdays at 20.00
After dusk, the historic neighborhood of Neve Tzedek and Rothschild Boulevard is suddenly very different from what you have seen during the day: many bars and restaurants surface. The guides will show you their preferred places and give you interesting background information about the architecture, the people, the nightlife and life in Tel Aviv in general.

3.) Meeting point: where Rothschild Boulevard meets Herzl St.

Old Jaffa: Wednesdays at 10.00
During this walk, you will explore the famous flea market and go up to St. Peter's

Church, pass mosques, street vendors, go over the Zodiac Bridge and discover the small medieval alleys of Jaffa with its artists and galleries.

4.) Meeting point: Tourist information at Marzuk & Azar St. (near Clock Tower)

The White City: Saturdays at 11.00
The tour goes up Rothschild Boulevard and explores the side streets. By strolling up the green boulevard, you will learn about the beginnings of Tel Aviv, the architecture, the city's UNESCO status and the city development of then and now.

5.) Meeting point: 46, Rothschild Boulevard (corner of Shadal St.)

5.3 City Walks

5.3.1 From Neve Tzedek to Achuzat Beit

At the end of the 19th century, Jaffa started to blossom. The already overpopulated medieval town with its narrow alleys was about to collapse. The demand for flats was very high and the level of hygiene very low. Living in Jaffa would soon turn into a realistic threat to one's health. Under the auspices of Shimon Rokach, Aaron Chelouche (many times transcribed from Hebrew as Shlush), Haim Amzaleg and Zera Barnet, a group of 48 families started a new settlement outside Jaffa. They bought land north-west of Jaffa and founded the first Jewish suburb in 1887 – Neve Tzedek, Oasis of Justice.

The Neve Tzedek neighborhood with its low-rise buildings and the red roofs has maintained (so far) its village character and most of the buildings are still in the original state. This area is full of galleries, museums, restaurants, cafés, bars and little shops. Coming from Jaffa, Neve Tzedek is on the way to Achuzat Beit (original name of Tel Aviv.) If you want to follow the chronological city development, it is best to start at the old railway station, HaTachana, with Jaffa in the back. This is how the founders saw it. On the way to the north, you will discover the little side streets where even today there is no side-walk and time seems to stand still, like in Sharabi Street (extension of Lilienblum Street.) When you have reached the Eden Cinema, you are standing on the border of Neve Tzedek and Achuzat Beit, later re-named Tel Aviv.

1) The old train station – HaTachana
The old train station of Jaffa – HaTachana – is located on the border to Neve Tzedek. The construction of the railway strengthened Jaffa's position as the economic center of Palestine; in 1892, the first train would run between Jaffa and Jerusalem. In the last years, the station has been thoroughly renovated and stylish boutiques, cafés and restaurants moved into the old buildings. Next door, you find the museum of the Ministry of Defense.

2) Suzanne Dellal Center (6, Yehieli St.)
In the core of Neve Tzedek, you find this dance center in a palace-like setting. Founded in 1989, Dellal organizes today over 750 events throughout the year and is renowned for its modern interpretations. The center is home to different dance companies, like the "Batsheba Dance Company" or the "Inbal Dance Theater."

3) Mosaic
A big mosaic has been dedicated to the founding fathers of Neve Tzedek at the exit of the Dellal Center.

4) The Chelouche House (32, Shlush St.)

Aaron Chelouche (1829-1920) was one of the founding fathers. He had come from Algeria to Palestine and was an influential member of the society. Last but not least, his knowledge of Arabic came in very handy when buying plots of land. His house on 32, Shlush Street was completed in 1886.

5) Shai Agnon's House (2, Rokach St./ 35, Shlush St.)

Nobel Prize winner Shmuel Yosef Agnon (1888-1970) lived in this house from 1909 to 1913. He wrote poetry and short stories in Hebrew and Yiddish in which he portrayed Jewish life in the East-European "Shtetls." In 1966, he had been awarded the Nobel Prize for literature together with the Jewish German writer Nelly Sachs.

6) Amzaleg Haus (22, Shlush St.)

This beautiful entrance leads to the house of Haim Amzaleg (1824-1916) who was not only one of the co-founders of Neve Tzedek, but also British vice consul in Jaffa during the reign of the Ottomans (until 1917.) As British citizen, Amzaleg could easily circumvent the law that prohibited the sale of land to Jews. As a British diplomat, he signed the purchase of several hectares of land about 15 km south of Jaffa that he would later sign over to Jewish families. Because of this, 17 Jewish families could lay the corner stone of the city of Rishon Le Zion.

7) The Chelouche Bridge

Aaron Chelouche was the builder of this bridge that once crossed the railway and connected Jaffa and Neve Tzedek.

8) Neve Tzedek Tower (65, Eilat St.)

The construction of the Neve Tzedek Tower made it finally obvious that the "Oasis of Justice" (as Neve Tzedek is translated from Hebrew) will not be able to preserve its village character forever. Several neighborhood groups have been founded to prevent similar projects in the future. Time will tell if that is possible.

9) Walhalla, the Wagner factory

Right next to the Neve Tzedek Tower, there are two little buildings from the Templers, some of the last remaining from the Walhalla settlement that was established here in 1888. When Jaffa started expanding during the economic boom, the Templers also kept an eye out for new plots. Some of the families settled their houses and garages on the border between Neve Tzedek and Jaffa, close to the railway, like Wilhelm and Georg Wagner who produced water pumps.

The Wagner family was one of those Templers who were allowed to re-open their factories after the end of World War II. The Jews were indignant. After the war, the truth about the Nazis had been known to the world. In 1946, Gotthilf Wagner was murdered on Levanda Street in Tel Aviv. The murder case has never been solved, but a Jewish resistance group had been suspected.

10) The Lorenz Café (57, Eilat St.)
The Templer Society of Walhalla had a very lively social life. In No. 57, there used to be the Lorenz Café. Legend has it that this was a popular venue for the meetings of the Rotary Club and that it was the best place to enjoy a draught beer. The Templers were German patriots and were strongly and increasingly infiltrated by the Nazis who would also gather at the Lorenz since the end of the 1920s. In 1925, the Kessem Cinema started showing movies here. With its location on the Jaffa side of town, it was the only competition to the Eden Cinema that had the only concession for Tel Aviv (see "Eden Cinema.")

Since 1970, the building was abandoned. The Schechter Institute for Jewish Culture purchased it in 2011 and completed the renovations in 2012.

11) Former German Consulate (59, Eilat St.)
The German Consulate was located right next to the Lorenz until the beginning of World War II. The proximity to the Templers in Walhalla and the Arabs in Jaffa was of strategic importance for the Nazis in Palestine.

12) The Writer's House (21, Shimon Rokach St.)
Built in 1887, it used to be the seat of the newspaper, HaPoel HaZair. After a successful fight against its demolition, it finally became a museum. It poses many works from Nachum Gutman (1898-1980) who was also famous for his prose, children's books and illustrations. A big mosaic of his is displayed in the hall of the Shalom Tower.

13) The Rokach House (36, Shimon Rokach St.)
Shimon Rokach, one of the founding fathers of Neve Tzedek, built this building in 1887. This house, with its unusual roof, was the first that was finished in the new settlement outside Jaffa. Here, it was his grand-daughter, the sculptor Leah Majaro-Mintz, who prevented it from being torn down. She refurbished the building and opened it later for exhibitions.

14) The Twin Houses (32, Pines St.)
Aaron Chelouche built for his two sons two identical buildings at 30-32, Pines St.; they are called "The Twins."

15) The Eden Cinema (Lilienblum St./ Pines St.)

When the Eden Cinema opened in 1914, the neighbors were not amused. They wrote aggressive letters to the municipality claiming that a place of public entertainment would bring the neighborhood down. The operators, Moshe Abarbanel and Mordechai Weiser, had the exclusive license for the local cinema business for the next 15 years. Nevertheless, another movie theater was opened in 1920 in 57, Eilat Street (10.) Since this was right on the border but officially Jaffa, it did not interfere with the exclusive license for Tel Aviv. The Eden Cinema started with silent films. It was the first movie theater in the country and very successful. Later, an open air movie theater was added and the locals distinguished between the summer- and the winter-Eden. The Eden operated until 1974. The building is protected.

5.3.2 From Achuzat Beit to Tel Aviv

Under the auspices of Akiva Aryé Weiss, the society "Achuzat Beit" was founded in 1906; a housing company to develop the new settlement the European Zionists were dreaming of. On 11 April 1909, the purchased plots were divided into lots and construction began. In 1910, the name was changed to "Tel Aviv", this was the title Nachum Sokolow had given the Hebrew translation of Herzl's "Altneuland." In the same year, the "Street of the People" – Ha'am Street – was renamed Rothschild Boulevard. Baron Edmond de Rothschild had supported the project financially.

The corner of Herzl Street and Rothschild Boulevard is a good starting point for a discovery walk through the former Achuzat Beit; this is where everything had begun. Herzl Street was the first commercial street while the Boulevard was the place where the founders erected their individual villas in the Eclectic Style. This was the main building style in Achuzat Beit; a bit of the Near East (many houses had orient-style windows) and some decorative elements from the home country (like little Russian towers.) The architecture will change little by little on the way up to the north-east. Take a journey through time from 1909, the year of the groundbreaking, until 1957, when the Friedrich Mann Auditorium was inaugurated.

1) The First Kiosk (Herzl St./ Rothschild Blvd.)
The journey starts at the first kiosk of Tel Aviv. Today, you will see a replica there and the main part of the Boulevard is now home to little bars, cafés and tapas bars that operate from similar kiosks.

2) The Weiss House (2, Ahad Ha'am St./ Herzl St.)
The house of the Achuzat Beit founding father, Aryé Akiva Weiss, was the first in the new settlement. In the following decades, the house would be altered inside and outside. In the 1920s, another floor was added to the originally single-storied house for residential use by the Weiss family. The ground floor was used commercially. Also the façade was changed over the years. The original design wasn't discovered until the whole building was refurbished in the year 2000.

3) Migdal Shalom/ Gymnasium Herzliya (9, Ahad Ha'am St.)
The Shalom Tower is a controversial office building that can be seen from far away. When it was finished in 1965, it was the highest building in Israel and for a long time in the whole Near East. On 28 July 1909, the cornerstone was laid for the first Hebrew high school in the world– the "Gymnasium Herzliya." Legend has it that architect Joseph Barky had been inspired by the Holy Temple in Jerusalem which led to the Moorish design. In the first years after the founding of the high school in 1906, the students of Yehuda Levi Metman-Cohen (1869-1939) and his wife, Fania, were educated in their private flat in Jaffa. In 1963, the Gymnasium Herzliya moved

to a new building in Jabotinsky Street where today an ornamented iron gate commemorates the school's first building from 1909. The first building had been built on a hill and embodied the values of a new Jewish society: no longer as a house of prayer or the center of daily life, but as a house of culture and education.

On the ground floor and the first floor, there is a public exhibition about the first days of Tel Aviv. Even though the documentation is in Hebrew, the old photographs are well worth seeing. The entrance hall displays mosaics of Israeli artists, Nachum Gutman and David Sharir, which tell the city's history.

4) The First Department Store (16, Herzl St.)
Yehuda Magidovitch built here Tel Aviv's first department store in 1925, and the style is very characteristic of the 1920s. On the upper side of the façade, the old name can still be read: "Pensak's Passage."

5) The Shiff House (26, Lilienblum St. / Herzl St.)
Olga and Itzhak Frank built this building in 1909, and in those days it was the "Frank House" as it is noted in the archives. Like most buildings of that time, also the Frank House was not higher than one floor and had a red tiled roof. Later, in the 1920s, the Shiff family bought it, modified it like the Weiss House and also added another storey. Today, the Shiff House is the private bank museum of Bank Diskont which refurbished the building in 2006.

6) Memorial to the Founding Fathers
The memorial at the fountain is dedicated to the first 66 families of the city and was inaugurated in 1951. They had been the initiators who divided the purchased plots among each other on 11 April 1909, and hence led the cornerstone of Tel Aviv. The east side of Aharon Priver's memorial tells the city's history: the planning of the sand dunes, the Rothschild Boulevard and on the upper end, you will discover Dizengoff Square with its surrounding buildings in the International Style. The other side lists the names of the above mentioned 66 families.

7) Independence Hall (16, Rothschild Blvd.)

On 5 Iyar 5708 (14 May 1948), David Ben-Gurion proclaimed the State of Israel at Rothschild Boulevard. The first mayor of Tel Aviv, Meir Dizengoff, had left this private building of his to the municipality. Today, it is called "Independence Hall" and hosts the museum of the historic events that led to the foundation of the state. The statue in front of the building shows Meir Dizengoff on his horse.

8) The Golomb House (23, Rothschild Blvd.)

This building is from 1913. The owner, Eliyahu Golomb, was the founder of the resistance group, Hagana, and lived here until his death in 1945. At the beginning of the 1960s, the building was taken over by the Ministry of Defense and is today the Hagana Museum.

9) The Lederberg House (29, Rothschild Blvd./ Allenby St.)

Like many other buildings from the 1920s, the Lederberg House was also erected in the Eclectic Style. The façade displays ceramics with biblical themes. Downstairs, the legendary "Benedict's" serves one of the best breakfasts in town.

10) Allenby Street

In the days when Tel Aviv was booming, Allenby Street became increasingly important as the new commercial center. According to the city development, Allenby Street would also grow longer. The street starts south of Rothschild Boulevard and drops to the sea right behind the Yemenite Quarter. It gave the residents access to the beach without having to traverse the Arabic neighborhood of Manshiye (today Charles Clore Park.)

11) The Great Synagogue (110, Allenby St.)

The centers of the new Jewish society were cultural buildings and not synagogues. Hence, the Great Synagogue opened its doors in 1926 a bit off the city's most important street. It is still Israel's biggest prayer house. The fast and unforeseen growth of the new settlement was disadvantageous for the congregation. Allenby Street would strengthen its position as a commercial center and the residents preferred living in the new residential area that mushroomed in the north. Over there, in the new streets, they would later open little prayer houses. The architect, Aryé Elhanani, was in charge of the building's renovation in 1969 when the new "coat" of pillars was also added. This paid homage to Oscar Niemeyer who had already invented a very similar design in the 1950s for the Ministry of Foreign Affairs in Brasilia.

12) The Palm Tree House (8, Nahalat Binyamin St.)

The "Beit HaDekel" was built in 1922 by architect Yehoshua Zvi Tabechnik. During the 1920s, the local architects were searching for a "Hebrew Style," hence, the Star of David on many buildings façades or balcony ornaments. Here, in No. 8, the menorah is the decorative Jewish element on the upper iron balconies.

13) Bialik Street

This is one of the most interesting streets in the center of Tel Aviv because of its many different building styles. Bialik and its side streets form together the UNESCO-defined Zone C of the World Heritage area. Here, you find the house of poet Haim Nahman Bialik (No. 22), the Reuben Museum (No. 14), the first city hall (No. 26) and last but not least, the Felicja Blumental Center (No. 26) which houses a comprehensive music library and frequently organizes concerts. On the way to Allenby Street, you will find more buildings from the 1930s in the International Style.

14) King Albert Square

At the junction of Nahmani and Melchett – King Albert Square – not only are streets coming together, but also different architecture styles. The Pagoda House from 1924 combines western and oriental elements, like the 21 Moorish arches. The

Shafran House on the corner of Melchett and Nahmani is a typical building for the Eclectic Style. Right on the other side of the street, a construction in the International Style shows up.

15) The Levin House (46, Rothschild Blvd./ Shadal St.)

Zvi Levin, a Lithuanian-born American, made his life-long dream come true when he immigrated to Palestine after retirement. He appointed Yehuda Magidovitch to build his house on Rothschild Boulevard and in 1924, he moved in and lived there until he died in 1935. The house resembled an Italian summer house with neo-classical elements, a popular style at the end of the 19th century. His family decided to go back to the US and sold the Levin House that later became an English school, then Hagana headquarters and finally it was used as the Russian Embassy. The Embassy left the building in 1953 after a bomb blast. Authorities suspected the attack to be a protest against persecution of Jews in Russia. At some point in the 1980s, the house was sold to Alfred Akirov who refurbished the building completely for which he received a construction permit from the municipality for the office tower behind the building. Until 2006, the Levin House was used by the Sotheby's auction house. Finally, it was sold to the founder of the Heseg Foundation who gives grants to students in Israel.

16) The Engel House (84, Rothschild Blvd.)

The Engel House is one of the prominent representatives of the "Modern Movement." It was the first building in Tel Aviv constructed on pillars, an element that reflects Le Corbusier's influence on local architecture. He was architect Ze'ev Rechter's mentor. When the building plots became scarce, pillar construction was the sophisticated answer to the question of how to maximize use of space without ignoring the mandatory green areas. The roof garden expressed the values of the workers' movement of the 1930s, a space to socialize for all neighbors. The floor plan revolves around a courtyard that opens to the neighboring Mazeh Street.

17) The Rubinsky House (65, Sheinkin St./ Gilboa St.)

With each step, the boulevard is now slowly changing its architecture and the International Style becomes predominant. Lucian Korngold was mentioned many times as the architect of this building but other sources refer to old documents in the archives that show the names of Marcusfeld & Karnovsky.

18) HaBima (HaBima Square)

HaBima is considered Israel's national theater. It was founded in 1913 in Russia and finally settled in 1931 in Tel Aviv. Its own building was finished in 1945 but the company already moved in before the end of construction. From 2007 to 2010, the building was refurbished and expanded. The original building consisted of a cylinder that now has been integrated into the new cube.

19) The Mann Auditorium (1, Huberman St.)

The architects Ze'ev Rechter as well as Dov Karmi and their respective teams had both sent their own proposals for the auditorium and were surely more than surprised when the jury announced that they want a combination of both and prompted them to work together. The project got funding from Frederic R. Mann (1904-1987) from Philadelphia, USA, an international sponsor of art and music projects. The building was completed in 1957 and is since then the home of the Israeli Philharmonic Orchestra. Unlike most public buildings at that time, the Mann Auditorium has no stairs in front of the entrance and seems to absorb the visitors.

5.3.3 Jaffa – The Bride of the Sea

The natural harbor had turned Jaffa already early in history into the economic center of the region and into the focus of many conquerors. Every one of them had left his mark in the city's architecture, like the Ottoman governor (1808-1818) Muhamman Abu-Nabbut who constantly constructed new buildings. Jaffa has always been the melting pot of different cultures and religions and this has not changed. Only about 100 years ago, those little streets were crowded and packed with residents and merchants; today, they are picturesque and home to galleries, restaurants and shops. There is not much left from the original Jaffa and its character. The urban alterations already started during the British Mandate. Streets like Mifrats Shlomo and Luis Pasteur were built in those days when the British tore down houses to widen the streets so they could be accessed with military vehicles. Thanks to a group of artists who would settle in Jaffa later in the 1960s and 1970s, at least a part of the town was preserved. Today, the Old Jaffa invites you to romantic walk in its historic streets.

A tour through Jaffa can be well combined with a visit to the Ilana Goor Museum (see "museums") or a stroll in the flea market (see "shopping"), and later you will have the chance to drop by Dr. Shakshuka (3, Beit Eshel St.) to try Israel's national dish: shakshuka.

1) The Clock Tower (Yefet St.)
The clock tower is legendary. It was built in 1906 by Turkish Sultan Abd-el Hamid II who wanted to modernize the country. Fixed hours were considered quite revolutionary in a time when the day was subdivided into dusk and dawn. The clock tower is the most popular meeting point in Jaffa.

2) Kishleh – The Ottoman Prison
The prison of the old Saray (kishleh) was separated from the Saray in 1870 and relocated west of the clock tower. After 1948, it was used as police station until 2006. Currently, there is a hotel project being planned for future use. The relocation of the kishleh happened in a time when Jaffa was growing and the city walls were torn down to help the city expand.

3) The New Saray
At the end of the 19th century, the new Saray was completed, vis-à-vis the kishleh and the Ottoman administration closed the old Saray and moved to the new location. The white ruins are a reconstruction of the original neo-classical building that was bombed during the war of independence on 4 January 1948. Now it is the address of the Kishleh Hotel from the Orchid-Group.

4) Sabil Suleiman (Yefet St. at the Clock Tower)
A "sabil" is a public water place either for a ritual washing before the prayers or to refresh after a long journey. Sabil Suleiman was built in 1809 by Suleiman Pasha, the governor of Akko and "boss" of Muhammad Abu-Nabbut. It is located at the southern wall of the Mahmoudiya Mosque.

5) House of the Turkish Governor
The building on the right side of the Saray is the former building of the Turkish governor. During recent years, a concept had been developed to turn the building into a Turkish culture center. The works had already started when in 2010 the diplomatic relations between Israel and Turkey tensed and the project had been adjourned indefinitely due to the Gaza flotilla.

6) The Mahmoudiya Mosque (Roslan St.)
The Mahmoudiya Mosque, built in 1812 by governor Muhammad Abu-Nabbut, is the biggest in the city. Water reservoirs were installed in front of the mosque for the ritual washing. The hidden treasures of the mosque with its courtyards are not accessible for tourists since the mosque is not open for non-Muslim visitors.

7) The Flea Market
A visit to the flea market of Jaffa is a "must." The entrance can be easily found; it is the 2nd street on the left coming up from the clock tower, Oley Zion. In the streets around the flea market, young Israeli designers have their boutiques and ateliers. Not only is the flea market a paradise for bargain hunters, there are more second-hand and antique shops in the neighborhood as well as carpet and silver merchants. You will hear full-throated bargaining left and right; welcome to the Near East! Inside the shops it is a bit quieter, but nowhere else in the cities of Europe and Near East are neighbors so close. The whole area around the flea market is a little vibrant world spiced with nice cafés and restaurants.

8) The Old Saray (8-10, Mifrats Shlomo St.)
In the 19th century, Muhammad Abu-Nabbut expanded the old Saray that was originally built in 1740. It used to be part of a huge administrative structure that once also included a prison and a public bath house. The Ottomans used the building for about 150 years until they moved into a new Saray in 1890 next to the house of the Turkish governor.

9) The Andromeda Rock
This famous rock is located right next to the port of Old Jaffa and can be spotted from the boardwalk. According to the Greek mythology, Andromeda was the daughter of Egyptian king Cepheus and the Ethiopian queen Cassiopeia. She was

tied to the rock to be sacrificed to the sea but was rescued by her future husband, Perseus.

10) St. Peter
The Franciscan church was inaugurated in 1894 after several years of construction. The church is located pictorially on a hill and is the center of attraction for all visitors. The inside is abundantly decorated and the windows are especially well worth seeing. It also houses a painting of St. Peter on the roof of Simon the Tanner whose house is located nearby (19.)

11) Jaffa Visitors' Center
You will find the entrance to the underground visitors' center of Jaffa at Kedumim Square in front of St. Peter's Church. The center is located close to an archeological excavation and shows the long history of Jaffa (http://www.oldjaffa.co.il)

12) Gan HaPisga
The park on the hill (pisga = peak) with its exotic plants and several sculptures is the work of Avarahm Karavan. The "Statue of Faith" by Daniel Kafri and the "Zodiac Bridge" are popular photo motifs. The view from the top is worth the effort.

13) Zodiac Bridge
The balustrade of this short wooden bridge is decorated with the 12 signs of the zodiac. Put your hand on your sign and make a wish!

14) Statue of Faith (Gan HaPisga)
Israeli artist Daniel Kafri created this 4 meter high gate-resembling statue in 1977. It shows the three patriarchs Abraham, Isaac and Jacob in different biblical moments: Jacob's dream in which the land is promised to his descendents (left), Abraham's sacrifice of Isaac (right) and the fall of Jericho (top).

15) Ramses II's Gate Garden (Gan Sha'ar Ramses)
On the hill of Gan HaPisga you also find the Gate of Ramses II (1,400-1,200 BC) that was discovered during an excavation. This gate shows again the rich history of Jaffa and the political interests of the many conquerors who came here.

16) The Al-Bahr Mosque
The oldest mosque of Jaffa looks back on over 400 years of history; the year of construction is unknown but is estimated to be in the middle of the 16th century. Apparently, the mosque was constructed in different stages and the minaret added

at a later time. Legend has it that the wives of the fishermen came here to pray for their safe return. After years without usage, the building was refurbished in 1997.

17) Jaffa Port

This harbor is one of the oldest in the world and soaked with history. Pilgrims, crusaders, Jewish immigrants, Arab refugees — they all passed the port of Jaffa as well as countless boxes of Jaffa oranges. In 1936, this port would have to face competition for the first time in its history: the Jews built their own harbor in Tel Aviv close to the Yarkon river. Additionally, a modern harbor opened in 1965 in Ashkelon and Jaffa became quiet . Even though the big ships stay away from Jaffa, a new vibe has been emerging. Galleries and restaurants have reanimated the old port, fishermen are now selling fresh fish here and yachts are offered for sailing trips.

18) Netiv HaMazalot St.

The street of the signs of the zodiac, Netiv HaMazalot, runs parallel to the port. From here you can walk up to the old city with its narrow little streets. Many of them are named after the signs: Tleh (Aries), Shor (Taurus), Teomim (Gemini), Sartan (Cancer), Aryé (Leo), Betula (Virgo), Moznaim (Libra), Akrab (Scorpio), Keshet (Sagittarius), Gdi (Capricorn), Dli (Aquarius), Dagim (Pisces.)

19) Simon the Tanner (Shimon Habourskai St.)

He belongs to the Saints of the Maronite Christian faith and is mentioned in the Acts of the Apostles (9 and 10). According to the Acts, Simon was the landlord of St. Peter. On his rooftop, Peter had a vision that sent him to Caesarea to meet Captain Cornelius, a non-Jew. This is the first biblical hint to an early Christian expansion of the missionary activities outside the Jewish community. This exegesis is debatable as is the location. This house can best be reached once you pass St. Peter's at the end of Kedumim Square. It has been in the possession of the Armenian-Christian family Zarkarian for several generations.

20) The Libyan Synagogue (2, Mazal Dagim St.)

House number 2 is located at the western end of Mazal Dagim Street. When finished in 1749, the building was used as a caravansary and offered accommodation for travelers and their animals. In the Ottoman empire, these places were much more modest than in other parts of the orient; you would even have had to bring your own cutlery and blankets. From 1860 onwards, the building was used by the local population for different purposes. Rabbi Zunana purchased it later to found here a synagogue with a hostel for Jewish pilgrims. The exact year is not known. Years later, the Jews were expelled and were only allowed to pray there when the Arab owner granted them permission. After 1948, the synagogue was given back to the Libyan Jewish congregation. Nowadays, it is only frequented for special events.

21) The Floating Orange (Mazal Aryé St.)

At the eastern end of Mazal Aryé Street, after passing the Richter Art Gallery (No. 24), you will see this exceptional installation: an orange tree floating above the earth. With this work, the artist Ran Morin presents the fusion of nature and technology.

22) St. Georgius (1-5, Louis Pasteur St.)

This Greek Orthodox church from the 19th century is located right on the border with Ajami where Christians from the Near East settled down at the end of the 19th century.

הרובע המרוני
MARONITE QUARTER
حي الماروني

5.3.4 Ajami

At the end of the 19th century, Jaffa was booming. The economy was strong and there were plans being made for a railway to Jerusalem. It had become crowded in Jaffa, flats were scarce and the expansion of the city became an imperative. Starting in 1870, little by little, the city wall was torn down. The Jews founded Neve Tzedek, the Muslims Manshiye and the Christians went south and settled eventually in Ajami, next to the Muslim neighborhood of al-Jabaliya. On the western side of Yefet Street, the Maronites founded their quarter; on the eastern side, the Copts.

During the War of Independence in 1947/48, most of the Arab citizens of Jaffa left the country and the neighborhood was deserted. With the founding of the State of Israel, Jews got expelled from Arabic states and many found a new home where somebody else had abandoned it. Arabs from other parts of Israel who had not left the country also moved to this area. Over the decades, Ajami got very run-down; the new big beach park, Gan HaMidron, was a dumping place and blocked the view to the sea until recently. The architectonic wealth of the neighborhood was not discovered until the 1980s when investors suddenly had an eye on Ajami and its old villas and palace-like old buildings. New, mainly Jewish neighbors moved in. Since then, the development of the neighborhood has been under fire for its increasing number of luxury condominiums which lead to a further scarcity in affordable flats.

Ajami is located in Jaffa's south. You can discover the Christian neighborhood by entering Ajami in the north and finish at the Givat Aliya Beach from where you can walk back to Jaffa next to the seaside. If you are too tired for a walk, you can also take bus No. 37 that stops above the Peres Peace Center. It will take you back to the Jaffa harbor and continue via Jerusalem Boulevard to the Carmel Market in Tel Aviv. The north-bound bus stop is on Valencia Street (becomes Ibn Sina Street) which is parallel to Kedem Street where the bus stop for the southern route is located.

1) Dolphin Street

Fortified by a hearty breakfast at "Abu Hassan Hummus" (at No. 1) you can now set out on a tour through Ajami. Be there early; once the hummus is sold, the shop closes. Dolphin Street is part of the Maronite Ajami. You will pass an Italian church (at No. 11) that is currently not in use and the Maronite church (at No. 20) which was built by church member Iksander Awad (also known as Alexander Howard) who is buried in the church's court yard.

2) Ytzhak Avineri Street

This street is worth a little detour. In 1855, the Coptic church founded a monastery here. At the intersection of Avineri and Yefet Street (at No. 51), you will see the

Catholic St. Anthony's church from 1932 and the neighboring Terra Santa High School. In the immediate proximity, you'll find the Anglican church (Yefet St. 48), also currently not in use.

3) Bathsheba de Rothschild St.
This little side street is hiding at the end the "Scot's House", an old English hospital from the 19th century. In the 1950s, it was closed and later acquired by two Scotsmen who turned it into a hotel. Nowadays, it can be rented for private events.

4) Sha'arei Nikanoor St./ Ziona Tagger St.
Left and right of Yefet Street, you will discover beautiful old houses. At Ziona Tagger Street No. 6, you see a building that belonged to a rich Arab family. The building style is called "Liwan house." These buildings consist of a big residential area in the middle of the house and various rooms are organized around it. When you cross Yefet Street, make you sure you go by Fakhri Geday's pharmacy at No. 65. This is a true example of the old Jaffa before 1948. The Geday family has been living in Jaffa for many generations and always owned this place.

5) Dudaim St./ Lotus St.
The streets east of Yefet, Dudaim and Tsonobar Street, are well worth a stroll. Magnificent buildings in different architecture styles are waiting for you.

6) 80, Shivte Yisrael St.
This building is very typical of the Jaffa building style of the 19th century: a palace-like generous and elegant structure with inner balconies and decorated pillars. A "Liwan".

7) Toulouse St. 1

Architect Yitzhak Rapaport built this modern building in 1935 for a wealthy Arab family who left the country in 1948. With the architect as mediator, they were able to sell the building to the French Republic before leaving. Since then, it is the residence of the French ambassador to Israel.

8) Givat Aliya Beach

This is the southernmost beach of Tel Aviv. The atmosphere is relaxed and the panorama very different from all the other beaches; to the north there is Jaffa, to the south, Bat Yam. The sea here is rough and the ground rocky; not the best place for a swim, but definitely for a long beach walk. Several good restaurants with Arabic cuisine can be found in proximity to the beach as well as Jaffa Slope Park that connects this beach with the port.

9) Peres Center for Peace (132, Kedem St.)

This impressive building is a direct neighbor of the Givat Aliya Beach. It seems as if it was contemplating the sea. The massive cube is the design of the Italian architects Massimiliano & Doriana Fuksas and was completed in 2009 after 6 years of construction. The NGO in the Peres Peace Center was founded in 1996 by Israel's President Shimon Peres. The organization supports the dialogue between Jews and Arabs and operates in many fields; in nearly all areas of society, the organization offers help and cooperation: medical services, education, technology, economy, etc. The NGO's philosophy is that peace only happens between people and not organizations.

10) Gan HaMidron

This park of approximately 50 hectares is the second biggest of Israel after Yarkon Park and is one of the most comprehensive recycling projects. Nothing seems to remind the visitor of the city's dumping ground that was here until 2010. Today, you see a green oasis next to the sea, ideal for jogging and biking and equipped with nice playgrounds. The park connects Jaffa with the Givat Aliya beach, the ultimate place for a beach walk.

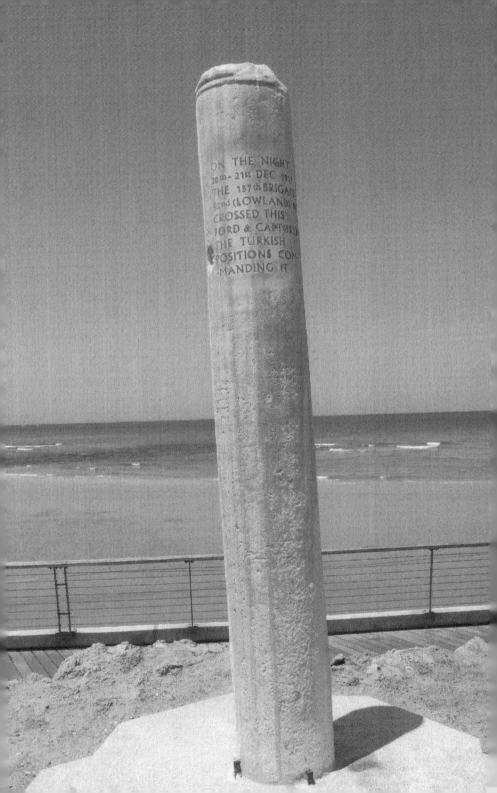

5.3.5 Historic Beach Walk

Walking along Tel Aviv's beaches is also a journey through the city's young history. It is convenient to walk the tayelet (Hebrew for "beach front") from south to north. This way, you follow the 100 years of city history chronologically and avoid sunburn.

1) HaTachana

The old train station of Jaffa, HaTachana, is the perfect start for a walk northward. Only a few years ago, this compound had been refurbished and built up again. It is located in the former district of Manshiye. Jaffa's position as the economic center of Palestine benefited significantly from the railway to Jerusalem. At the end of the 19th century, it started to expand. From 1870 on, the city walls were torn down to support the expansion. North of Jaffa, the new district of Manshiye was founded.

2) The Etzel House

The last survivors of Manshiye are the Etzel Museum across from the old train station, the "Red House" on the compound and last but not least, the Hassan Bek Mosque. After the ruins of Manshiye had been torn down in the 1960s, the plan was to turn this area into Tel Aviv's business district. But things changed, and today the Israeli economy is represented next to the Ayalon highway on the border to Ramat Gan in the east. Between 1947 and 1948, Jews and Arabs competed for dominance in Palestine. At the end of April 1948, the resistance group Irgun (Etzel) conquered Manshiye. The residents of Jaffa could see the explosions from far away. As a sign of victory, the Israeli flag was hoisted on top of the Hassan Bek Mosque. Manshiye was conquered.

3) The Charles Clore Park/ Manshiye

With the new plans for the future city development, the ruins of Manshiye were finally torn down and this district would totally be erased in 1963. In 1974, the Charles Clore Park was inaugurated and modernized in 2007. The name honors the British financier and philanthropist Charles Clore (1904-1979) whose investment group also included the English department store Selfridges. His "Clore Foundation" supports Jewish projects in Great Britain and abroad as well as museums and art collections.

4) The Hassan Bek Mosque

Hasan Bek became the new Ottoman mayor of Jaffa in the summer of 1914. The mosque of Manshiye that was built in 1916 is named after him. Later in history when the aggressions between Jews and Arabs were on the rise, there were repeated sniper attacks on Jews from the minaret of the mosque. The mosque had not been used for a long time and was finally given back to the Muslim community in 1980s. Today's minaret is double the height of the original which broke down in 1983.

5.) Delphinarium

For the Israeli society, the Dolphinarium remains a trauma. A tragedy happened here on 1 June 2003, when a suicide bomber attacked inside the discotheque. 21 people, mostly teenagers, died in the attack and 132 were injured. In front the Dolphinarium, a memorial stone in Hebrew, Russian and English remembers the victims. On the sign behind the stone, two young people are holding hand and the text says "We will not stop dancing.".

Even more than a decade later, there is still a website memorizing the victims (http://www.dolphi.org) as well as annual memorial services are held at the site. For years, the city hall wanted to tear down the dolphinarium. Now, the days of the building finally seem to be counted. In December 2014, a hotel project was approved to be built here within the next years.

6) Border Tel Aviv–Jaffa

During the British Mandate, Daniel Street was the border between Jaffa and Tel Aviv. On 1 May 1921, two Jewish groups violently clashed during Labor Day demonstrations. Both groups were knocking each other around when suddenly an Arab group gathered to beat up the Jews; the violence escalated and led to shootings. The civil population organized themselves and sealed off Tel Aviv. In the following days, they picked up the remaining Jews in Jaffa and cast out Arabs from Jewish neighborhoods. Daniel Street would repeatedly be the venue of conflicts between Jews and Arabs also later in history.

7) 1 Allenby Street/ Knesset Square/ Opera Tower

1 Allenby is an historic address. It used to be the seat of the Knesset (until 1 December 1949) and later of the Israeli National Opera (1958-1982.) The construction work for this building started in 1990 and its name is reminiscent of the golden times of the Israeli Opera and the square in front, reminiscent of the first year after the foundation of the State of Israel: the Opera Tower at Knesset Square. On 19 of 23 floors, there are luxury flats with a private pool on the rooftop. In the lower part of the building, there is a shopping mall with several movie theaters.

8) London Square

Right behind the Orchid Hotel, you will find a little garden with sculptures like ships. This is the memorial for the Aliya Bet (in Israel, "ha-apala"), the "illegal"

immigration of Jewish refugees. Historic photos and documentation explain the events. On the eve of the Reichskristallnacht – night of the broken glass – the government of the British Mandate published the 1939 White Paper that also contained the quota of Jewish refugees that were allowed to enter Palestine in the coming years. A subdivision of the HAGANA, Mossad le Aliya Bet, organized the clandestine immigration of Jewish refugees from Europe between 1938 and May, 1948. More than half of them were stopped by the British Navy. If they were lucky, they were sent mainly to refugee camps in Cyprus, but other ships were sent back to Europe, a death sentence for the passengers.

9.) DAN Hotel

The colorful façade is the curtain behind which hides a true German-Jewish success story: the former "Pension Käthe", a hostel owned by Käthe Danielewicz. Architect Lotte Cohen, originally from Berlin, had built Käthe's hostel here, a renowned accommodation in Tel Aviv with 21 rooms that was later sold to the Federmann brothers in 1947. They kept the name and built up a well-known hotel chain, Dan Hotels, with currently 14 hotel properties. Still today you can find the "KD" on the façade.

10.) Abie Nathan (south of the Renaissance Hotel)

Follow the beach walk downstairs, in the direction of the Renaissance Hotel. Shortly before you arrive at the hotel, you will find a little memorial plaque on the wall and a built-in loudspeaker. Abie Nathan (1927-2008) was an Israeli peace activist and founder of the radio station "Voice of Peace." On 28 February 1966, Nathan flew from Israel to Egypt with his own little plane – Shalom One – to present to President Nasser his ideas about peace talks between Israel and Egypt. He got arrested on his arrival and was sent back to Israel where he was arrested again, but later not sentenced. He kept on trying during the years of 1967 and 1968, and each time the Egyptians would send him back to Israel where he ultimately served a short prison sentence. In 1973, he bought a ship from which he operated the pirate station "Kol Shalom" (Voice of Peace.) Outside Israeli waters, he broadcasted pop music and got actively engaged for peace in the Near East. In 1978, he would repeatedly meet up with the PLO for which he also served a prison sentence in Israel. The radio station was very popular but had to close down on 1 October 1993 due to financial difficulties. Abie Nathan received the International Human Rights Award of Nuremberg in 1997. An online radio station has picked up Nathan's idea and created an acoustic memorial for him: http://www.thevoiceofpeace.co.il .

11) Wall Paintings Gordon Pool
Close to Gordon Street, the walls at the beach front are decorated with nice paintings of bathers. This is where the first swimming pool of Tel Aviv had been, the Gordon Pool. The new pool is located a bit further north.

12.) Arlozorov Memorial
Across from the entrance of the Carlton Hotel, you will see a green tarnished sculpture in memory of Chaim Arlozorov (1899-1933.) The Arlozorovs were

Ukrainian Jews who had immigrated to Germany in 1905. Chaim and his parents had lived in Eisenacher Straße in Berlin-Kreuzberg. He had been fascinated by Zionism but until his permanent move to Palestine in 1924, he had been very close to the woman who would later be known as Magda Goebbels (maiden name: Behrend.) Once in Palestine, he climbed the social ladder and became the head of the Mapai party and the right hand of Chaim Weitzman. After a dinner with his wife in the Dan Hotel, Arlozorov was shot at the beach of Tel Aviv in June 1933. This murder had never been solved. In recent years, researchers uttered suspicions that the clues could lead to Germany and that this contract murder might have been the revenge of an unfulfilled love (see: "Qui a tué Arlozoroff" by Tobie Nathan, published so far only in French, ISBN-13: 978-2246751311)

13.) Independence Park / Gan HaAtzmaut
From the hill next to the Hilton Hotel, this little park overlooks the sea. It is a nice spot for a romantic sunset. In 1952, the park was offered to the municipality by a private person. Finally in 2009, the area was refurbished for the 100-year celebration of Tel Aviv. Today, the park is home to several sculptures and a little playground.

14) Tel Aviv Port

A new harbor was another significant step towards independence and construction started on 17 May 1936. Between Haifa and Jaffa, there was no other port until then. The coast was very shallow and big ships came as close as they could, but passengers and goods had to be brought ashore by rowboats. The local economy boomed and at the same time more and more immigrants came from Europe; unloading a ship took longer each time and sometimes the ships would have to wait for days until they got unloaded. By 1949, the municipality decided to expand the port activities and deepened the harbor to allow the ship to land and stop the unloading at sea. Today the port is an attractive place with good restaurants, coffee shops and a buzzing nightlife.

15) The Yarkon Estuary

The Yarkon River presented a natural barrier in the fight between the British and the Ottomans. In the night of 20/21 December 1917, the British troops crossed the river and defeated the enemy by surprise. Because of the flood, the Turks had felt secure on the other side. Close to the lighthouse ruins, a stone column is reminiscent of this event.

16) The Lighthouse

On 13 December 1934, two ships collided in front of the Jaffa port. Soon after this accident, this lighthouse was constructed, starting in January 1935, to improve the situation at the shallow coast.

17) The Reading PowerStation

The red lights of the Reading power plant are very visible at night. For a long time, this was the northern end of Tel Aviv until the expansion beyond the Yarkon River. The newly constructed beachfront of Reading passes the airport of Sadeh Dov.

18.) Airport Sadeh Dov

With the intensifying conflict between Arabs and Jews, it became increasingly dangerous for Jews to travel outside the city. The then-mayor of Tel Aviv, Israel Rokach, asked the Mandate government for permission to build Tel Aviv's own airport. Sadeh Dov was finished in 1938 and offered regular flights to Haifa. The airport still serves national flights and is also used by the military, but those days are counted. The military announced the closing of the airport for end of 2015, two years earlier than planned, to give way for the construction of new flats. We will see.

5.4 Further Places of Interest

If you have some time left in Tel Aviv, the following places might be of interest to you. They are listed from south to north.

1) American-German Colony

In September 1866, George Jones Adams, the founder of the "Church of the Messiah", and his 156 followers had come from Boston to Jaffa. They bought a plot of land and erected the wooden prefabricated houses they had brought from home. None of them had been prepared for the hardship of agricultural life abroad and only a few months later, in winter 1867, most of them wanted to leave Jaffa and go back home. The majority of them had already left when in the beginning of 1869, some southern German "Templers" arrived and offered to buy their settlement that would later be known as the "(American-) German Colony of Jaffa." Today, there are only two streets left with houses from that time: Bar Hoffman and Auerbach Street. The Templers founded a new settlement east of Jaffa in 1871, Sarona. At the same time, there were plans to open a railway connection from Jaffa to Jerusalem and in 1888, the Templers added another little compound close to the future train station, Walhalla. The railway line was opened in 1892.

2) Beit Immanuel (8, Auerbach St.)

During the times of the Templers, the Beit Immanuel was their parish hall. In 1878, they sold it to Baron Plato von Ustinov, the grandfather of actor Peter von Ustinov. He renovated and expanded the building where in 1895 his sister-in-law started operating the luxury Hôtel du Parc. German Emperor Wilhelm II is also reported to have chosen this hotel when he crossed Jaffa on his way to Jerusalem. The current congregation turned Beit Immanuel into a little historic museum and guest house.

3) Maine Friendship House (10, Auerbach St.)

The current owners, Dr. Reed and Jean Holmes, saved the building from being torn down. They opened a little museum that they also show to visitors who knock on their doors outside the official opening hours (Fridays 12.00-15.00, Saturdays 14.00-16.00, http://www.jaffacolony.com, Tel. 03-681.9225)

4) Immanuel Church (15, Bar Hoffman St.)

The construction of the church happened thanks to protestant Baron Plato von Ustinov. It was inaugurated in 1904 and after 1948, handed over to the Norwegian Lutheran Church. Several congregations use the church which is open between Tuesdays and Fridays from 10.00 to 14.00. If you are interested in a group tour, the congregation will be happy to hear from you: immanueljaffa@gmail.com .

From here you can take bus No. 40 which stops in front of the Neve Tzedek Tower (other side of the street, direction north-east.) It brings you to the HaShalom train station at the Azrieli Center.

5) Azrieli Center (132, Menachem Begin St.)

The Azrieli Center is Israel's biggest shopping mall but not the country's highest building. This title goes to the Moshe Aviv Tower in Ramat Gan. However, the Azrieli Center has the highest viewing platform. From the 49th floor, you can see Ashkelon in the south, Hadera in the north and on clear days even Jerusalem in the east. Before going, please check with the calendar on their website since this popular venue is very often booked. On days of reduced opening hours, the entrance fee is reduced as well. The access to the platform is located on the 3rd floor. Tel. 03-608.1179, http://mitzpe49.co.il. Su.–Th. 09.30–00.00. Fr. 09.30–15.00. Sa. 10.00–00.00. Entrance fee: 15-22 NIS.

From here, you can walk to the Sarona settlement across the street.

6) Templer Settlement "Sarona"

During World War II, the British Mandate government had used the site partially for their own purposes, and nothing is left from the orchid and orange plantations that once surrounded the settlement. Only the southern part of the settlement is still there, south of Kaplan Street. The Templers had introduced effective agricultural methods with which they managed to harvest large quantities of oranges that were shipped to Europe and elsewhere. Thanks to the Templers, the famous Jaffa oranges became internationally known. The history of the Templers had been forgotten for a long time and new high-rise buildings were already planned when historians suddenly remembered the Templers. Locally, the area is known as HaKirya, the campus. It was the first seat of parliament of the young State of Israel, and the area north of Kaplan Street is still in public use. Since 2011, the area underwent renovation and in 2014 an "open air shopping village" with restaurants and shops was inaugurated.

The French professor Dr. Catherine Weill-Rochant wrote her doctoral thesis about the city development of Tel Aviv ("L'Atlas de Tel Aviv") and literally "stumbled" over something very interesting: the street map of Sarona looks very much like the one of Kirschenhardthof where the Templers had been founded in 1861. Even the street names were in German at that time. The Templers typically divided the settlements by two major streets and located at their junction the community buildings like the school, kindergarten and parish hall. The complete history of the German Templers in Sarona and the political background can be read in the chapter on urban history of Tel Aviv. Due to the renovation of the settlement and the preparations for the shopping village, some of the old buildings were removed from their original location and relocated closer to the other houses. If you keep following Kaplan Street westward, you will soon come by an interesting building façade on the right-hand side: at 11, Leonardo da Vinci Street, the city history is summarized in one single painting.

In order to continue further north, take bus No. 26 or 89 at Ibn Gvirol. Right next to the city hall is located the Yitzhak Rabin Memorial.

7) The Yitzhak Rabin Memorial (71, Ibn Gvirol St.)

On 4 November 1995, Israel's President Yitzhak Rabin was murdered after a peace rally in front of the Tel Aviv city hall. The murderer, an orthodox Jew, later said he

 did it to protest against the peace agreement Rabin had signed with PLO leader Yasser Arafat. Right here the memorial was set up: 16 basalt stones from the Golan Heights were lowered into the ground and remind the visitor of an earthquake. This is exactly how the effect of the murder on the Israeli society was described later, an earthquake. On the wall next to the memorial, some graffiti was conserved from the days following the attack when thousands of Israelis mourned Rabin and lit candles. At this time, the square was still named Kikar Malchey Yisrael, Kings of Israel Square.

8.) Holocaust Memorial

The sculpture on Rabin Square, in front of the city hall, is a holocaust memorial that forms a star of David with its two triangles. The inside of the triangles hosts more metal work like the Hebrew word "yizcor", meaning memory. The artwork was created by Yigal Tumarkin. The Dresden born artist (* 1933) is the son of the later renowned East German director and actor Martin Hellberg. Tumarkin came to Israel at the age of two, together with his mother.

9.) Hechal Yehuda Synagogue (Ben Saruq St. 5)

Another name for this synagogue from 1980 is Seashell Synagogue. The construction was financially supported by the Recanati family, originally from Thessaloniki. Greek seashells are supposed to be the origin of inspiration for the building design that aims to commemorate the killing of the Jewish congregation of Thessaloniki during the Holocaust. The entrance is decorated with Jewish ornaments that were cut out of the concrete. Ben Saruq Street is located east of Ibn Gvirol between Jabotinski and Arolozorov. In immediate proximity, the Gymnasium Herzliya had found a new home (106, Jabotinski St./ Remez St.) after its original building was torn down in the early 1960s to build the Shalom Tower. The iron gate at the entrance shows a design that commemorates the original building of the world's first Hebrew High School in Achad Ha'am St.

5.5 Tel Aviv Beaches

The Hebrew word for beach is *chof*. The 16 *chofim* of Tel Aviv are extending over a length of 14 km. 13 of those beaches are located close to the city center and are listed below, from North to South. Each beach has not only its own name but also its own character. Most of the beaches provide gym facilities. Israelis love sports and are not shy to exercise in public. However, the favorite sport on the beach is not volleyball, but Matkot. Some love it; others would love to prohibit it. If you want to get a taste, you might want to watch the famous Israeli short film "Matkot - The End" (with English subtitles) on Youtube.

Tel Aviv's beaches are pretty clean and above all safe. Lifeguards are stationed at most beaches. Please pay attention to the flags. Red flag: there are strong currents and children and inexperienced swimmers should not go into the water; black flag: a general ban on swimming. At most of the beaches you can enjoy the free public Wi-Fi.

1.) Metzizim Beach
is located south of the port of Tel Aviv. There are volleyball courts, playgrounds, and a fitness facility. The Matkot player can be found even further south, near the religious beach.
The Metzizim Beach was formerly called the Sheraton Beach, but the Sheraton Hotel is now established closer to Gordon Beach. The current name, Metzizim, refers to an Israeli cult movie from the 70s.

2.) Nordau Beach/ Religious Beach (sex segregation)
Who would have thought that the very secular Tel Aviv would give public space to cater the needs of the orthodox community? Sundays, Tuesdays and Thursdays this section of the beach is for women only, Mondays, Wednesdays and Fridays for men. On Saturdays, it is open to the general public without segregation. On the women's days there is also a striking number of non-religious women coming (they are the ones with the sparse clothing) who want to sun-bathe undisturbed.

3.) Dog Beach
South of the orthodox community, the city's dogs and their owners are enjoying the sun. The dog beach appears to serve as a buffer between the orthodox and gay visitors. Israeli dogs are very social and well behaved in public. They enjoy the beach at least as much as their owners, and it is fun to watch them. The dog beach is the northern part of the famous Hilton Beach.

4.) Hilton Beach / Gay Beach at the Atzma-ut Park

Although this beach may have more gay visitors than other beaches, there is no reason not to bring children, quite the contrary. Many women come here because they feel they get chatted up less than on the other beaches; furthermore, the guests of the Hilton Hotel frequent this beach. A bit of caution is required at the southern end of this beach; surfers and kayakers are entering and leaving the sea in this area. The Hilton Beach ends at the Marina behind which you can find the Gordon salt water pool.

5.) Gordon Beach

starts right behind the Gordon salt water pool and has probably the highest density of foreign tourists. After all, there is one hotel next to the other. The beach is very nice and also public fitness facilities can be used.

6.) Frishman Beach

is not too different from Gordon Beach: much Matkot is played in little clothing. The beach-front restaurants offer great breakfasts in the morning.

7.) Bograshov Beach

is the third of the three beaches most frequented by tourists. Like Frishman and Gordon, also the Bograshov Beach is ideal to enjoy the sunset and have dinner in one of the beach restaurants or close by in the city center.

8.) Trumpledor Beach

is a much quieter spot than those beaches mentioned before. However, there are no lifeguards.

9.) Jerusalem Beach

Jerusalem Beach is situated vis-à-vis the Opera Tower. There are much less hotel towers than further north; hence the crowd is more local.

10.) Banana Beach oder Drummers' Beach

It is located north of the former dolphinarium (the ruins on the beach) and will probably experience a major change in the near future when the Dolphinarium will be torn down to build a new hotel. So far, Banana Beach is still there and it is best to visit on Friday afternoons or at sunset to enjoy the scenery and listen to the drummers. The atmosphere is relaxed.

11.) Alma Beach

Alma Beach is located close to the Charles Chlore Park. This is the only beach with a large green space nearby. Families love this place with its playgrounds. From here you have a beautiful view onto the old Jaffa.

The further you get to Jaffa, the less you will hear the typical noise of Matkot players and the more you will notice the smell and smoke of BBQ. While the Jews play Matkot on the beach, the Arabs prefer to have a BBQ on the lawn. If you do not want to do the cooking yourself, you can go to the nearby Manta Ray or cross the street to the old railway station HaTachana, where there are many restaurants and bars.

אפיפיטים

...ורים הטרופיים והסובטרופיים
שם הם מאבכססים גופי עצים
...ריס ...והשופים הם גדלים בס...
...יבה לכינידוק צמחים כראשם...
...גר ... נצעוך ... הנשאים עלים
...בים שרשי האיר הארוכם שכם
...שמשים ... גם כתאאיזה וכהבריטה
... מצטבר סביב שרתשים אלה
...רביטציה. או ... הם ... מטוטרפים
...המה רב .. שכבכבחית שכ חיים מחים
...מי הנגשם והספעם בכמסן הרוח
...דרן גא 8 ... טעבר כהסודרחמ

5.6   Botanical Garden

The Botanical Garden of the University of Tel Aviv allows visitors to get close to the still unanswered questions of science. Divided into 16 different areas - spread over 34,000 m² - the University shows amazing facets of their research, such as the root research in the Sarah Racine Root Laboratory. About half of the area belongs to Noah Naftulski garden for Israeli plants. The small country of Israel has several climatic regions like the Mediterranean, the desert or the mountain area and thus a variety of plant species. By walking through the cactus forest, the visitor learns how plants behave in arid and salt-rich regions on the different continents. Especially popular is the visit to the tropical house with its orchids, creepers and the humid tropical climate. The Botanical Garden does not not only serve as research field but also helps to preserve endangered plants.

The visit to the garden is free. If you are interested in a guided tour, please contact Campus Teva (in English nature): Tel. 03-640.5148, teva@tauex.tau.ac.il, http://www.campusteva.tau.ac.il

The Botanical Garden can be easily reached by bus 25 which runs every 15 minutes. It stops in front of the entrance, at gate 2 (bus stop "Bait Hatefuzot / Klausner St."). The Diaspora Museum (Bait Hatefuzot) is also located at this stop. The following is a selection of stops in the city center, where you can get on the bus (direction north!):

1.) Great Synagogue/ Allenby St. 110
2.) Carmel Markt/ Allenby St.
3.) King George/ HaHashmonaim (close to Gan Meir Park)
4.) King George/ Masrik Square
5.) Ibn Gvirol/ Rabin Square
6.) Ibn Gvirol/ Pinkas

Entrance:
7.) Klausner Street, vis-à-vis gate 2.

Opening hours: Su.-Th. 08.00-16.00, the tropical house closes at 14.30.

Entrance

1. Administration office,
classrooms and laboratories
2. Research grounds
3. Sara Racine Root Laboratory
4. Palm House
5. Daphna Carasso Tropical House
6. Shaded Fern Habitat
7. Ficus Collection
8. Succulents and Cacti
9. Lichens
10. Conifers
11. Manni-Elleren Garden of Utilitarian Plants
12. Garden of the Seven species
13. Menashe Garden of Medicinal Plants
14. Australian plants
15. Gate observatory
16. Mediterranean scrub observatory
17. Mediterranean scrub
18. Pine grove
19. Mediterranean shrubbery
20. Mediterranean batha
21. Wetland
22. Heavy soil
23. Semi-arid batha
24. Coastal sand-rock (kurkar)
25. Coastal dune
26. Desert vegetation
27. Oasis

toilets

6 Culture

6.1 Museums

Tel Aviv offers a much diversified range of museums and the local art scene, in particular, plays in the same league as those in big cosmopolitan cities. Even though these treasures are hidden behind unimpressive walls, the visitor soon will notice: Tel Aviv is shaking and something is moving! The museums of the neighboring cities bring the offer down to a round figure. This guide only lists the highlights in these other cities, not all the venues. They are only 5-10 km away from the center of Tel Aviv and can be reached by bus or taxi.

!!! The public and religious museums close on Friday in the early afternoon until Sunday. Museums that are open on Saturday normally close on Sunday.

In this book, the museums are subdivided into the following categories:

- City History
  - History of Tel Aviv Museum
  - Bauhaus Foundation
  - Shalom-Tower
- Pre-State-History
  - Independence Hall
  - ETZEL-Museum
  - HAGANA-Museum
  - LEHI-Museum
  - IDF-Museum
  - Jabotinsky Institute
  - Palmach-Museum
- Biographies
  - Ben-Gurion House
  - Bialik Museum
- Art Museums
  - Tel Aviv Museum of Art
  - Helena Rubinstein Pavilion for Contemporary Art
  - Ilana Goor Museum
  - Nachum Gutman Museum
  - Rokach Haus
  - Rubin Museum
- Religious Museums

- Beit Hatefutsot (House of the Diaspora)
- Israeli History and Culture
    - Eretz-Israel-Museum
    - Israel-Museum
- Museum in Ramat Gan
    - Harry Oppenheimer Diamond Museum
- Museums in Holon
    - Museum for Digital Art
    - Children's Museum
    - Cartoon Museum
    - Design Museum

6.1.1 City History

1.) The first city hall of Tel Aviv is now home to the new museum for urban history, the **Beit HaIr, History of Tel Aviv Museum**, inaugurated in 2009 for the city's 100th birthday. In preparation for Tel Aviv's 100th birthday celebration in 2009, many unique exhibits were collected that were reminiscent of the era before the proclamation of the state. The result is an extraordinary exhibition with old photo collections, films and the office of the first mayor, Meir Dizengoff, and interactive computer installations. 27, Bialik St., Tel. 03-724.0311, Mo.–Th. 09.00–17.00, We. 09.00-20.00, Fr.–Sa. + holidays 10.00–14.00, website only in Hebrew: http://www.beithair.org (only in Hebrew)

2.) The **Bauhaus Foundation** runs a small private museum that deals with the zeitgeist of the Bauhaus. The museum is primarily concerned with design furniture and everyday objects, not with architecture. The house itself was built in 1934 by architect Shlomo Gepstein for the Yaffe family and renovated in 1997 by Isaac B. Luxembourg. Bialik St. 21, Tel. 03-620.4664, Mi. 11.00-17.00, Fr. 10.00-14.00.

3.) There is hardly another building that has raised as much public dispute as the **Shalom Tower** (*migdal shalom*) Until 1958, the first Hebrew-speaking high school in the world – the Herzliya Gymnasium – was located here and the demolition of the historic building has been regretted many times ever since. When the Shalom Tower was inaugurated in 1965, it was Israel's highest building with 39 floors. The photo exhibition in the hall and on the first floor is well worth seeing, even though the texts are mainly in Hebrew, as are the famous mosaic works on the walls that tell the history of the city. 9, Achad Ha'am, Tel. 03-510.0337, Su.-Th. 08.00-19.00, Fr. 08.00-13.00. http://www.migdalshalom.co.il.

6.1.2 Pre-State-History

The historic museums in Israel are rather "political museums"; the country is young (founded in 1948) and its history is inseparably connected to the political events in the Near East. Politics are part of everyday life and if you want to understand Israel, then you might be interested in spending about an hour in the ETZEL museum at the Charles Clore Park (close to beach) where the events of 1947/48 are explicitly explained. The visitor will learn about the background of what still dominates the news today.

4.) **Independence Hall** is the name of the house where Israeli history was made. In this building, David Ben-Gurion proclaimed the State Israel on 5 Iyar 5708 (14 May 1948) only a couple of hours before the British left the country. The museum preserved everything exactly as it was: the same furniture and the same name tags on the reserved seats and many other exhibits that document the birth of the new state. Rothschild 16, Tel. 03-517.3942, Su.-Th. 09.00-17.00, Fr. 09.00-14.00. http://ihi.org.il, indbook@gmail.com

The Israeli Defense Forces (IDF) are in charge of 5 historic museums, of which 4 deal with the Jewish resistance groups ETZEL (also called "Irgun"), LEHI and HAGANA. The museums are: IDF History Museum, ETZEL Museum, LEHI Museum, HAGANA Museum and another extra ETZEL Museum that only deals with the War of Independence 1947/48 (at Charles Clore Park.) You can get a combined ticket for all those museums that is valid for one month.

!!! Make sure you bring your passport; access might be denied without it.

5.) The **ETZEL Museum** documents the activities of this resistance group who not only fought against the Arab attacks against Jews but also against the British who did not protect the Jews enough against the Arab assaults and would minimize Jewish immigration to Palestine during WWII; Jews were sent back to Europe which, for many, was a death sentence. The main goal of ETZEL was the establishment of a Jewish State within the territory of the British Mandate according to the Balfour Declaration of 1917.

The museum has two branches: a) 38, King George St. (close to Gan Meir Park and Dizengoff Square,) where the general history of the organization is exhibited, and b) at the beach on the way to Jaffa (Charles Clore Park, close to HaTachana, old train station) where only the events between 1947/48 are displayed in detail. 38, King George St., Tel. 03-528.4001, Charles Clore Park, Tel. 03-517.7180, both Su.-Th. 08.30–16.00.

6.) The HAGANA is the predecessor of the ZAHAL, the Israeli Army. The **HAGANA Museum** is located in the house of its founder Eliyahu Golomb and shows the evolution of the organization that initially had been founded for self-defense. In 1909, HaShomer (the watchman) was founded after several Arab assaults on Jews during the second Aliya between 1904 and 1914. From 1929 on, the HAGANA became the biggest and also technically best-equipped and experienced among the resistance groups. Like ETZEL, they also fought against the British and for more protection of the Palestinian Jews. During WWII, they organized the clandestine immigration of European Jews . Prominent members of the HAGANA included Yitzhak Rabin, Ariel Sharon and Dr. Ruth Westheimer. 23, Rothschild Blvd., Tel. 03-560.8624, Su.–Th. 08.30–16.00, hagana_museum@mod.gov.il

7.) The **Lehi Museum** – Beit Yair (or *House Stern*) is dedicated to Avraham Yair Stern and his resistance group LEHI during the time of the British Mandate (1918-1948.) LEHI had split from ETZEL and of all resistance groups, they were the most radical. The British had been their main enemy and to defeat them, they even considered collaborating with Nazi Germany and ultimately, also to bring the unwanted Jews from Europe to the Holy Land. 8, Stern St. , Tel. 03-682.0288, Su.–

Th. 08.30–16.00; http://www.lehi.org.il, lehi_museum@mod.gov.il

8.) The **IDF History Museum** (Israeli Defense Force) is a direct neighbor of the old train station HaTachana between Jaffa and Tel Aviv. The visit leads through 13 little halls and 6 small sites where history of the Israeli Army is documented with military uniforms, weapons, technical developments, files, videos and even a comprehensive tank exhibition. Tel Aviv Promenade (Tayelet), HaMered St./Yehezkel Kaufman St., Tel. 03-517.2913, Su.–Th. 08.30–15.30, toldot_zahal_museum@mod.gov.il

9.) The **Jabotinsky Institute** goes far beyond the biography of its founder Ze'ev Jabotinsky. Based on an imaginary conversation, Jabotinsky explains to his son the events happening at that time. The film "Af al pi chen" (Hebrew for Anyway) about the clandestine immigration from Europe, the so called Aliya Bet, is well worth watching. King George St. 38, 1st floor, Tel. 03- 528.6523, Su.-Th. 08.00-16.00 http://www.jabotinsky.org, office@jabotinsky.org

10.) The **Palmach Museum** is mentioned here for the sake of completeness. It is open to tourists, but a visit requires prior reservations. The tour takes 90 minutes and audio guides can be obtained in different languages. The Palmach was the Elite division of the HAGANA and very different from all the other groups. First of all they temporarily collaborated with the British, and all the members also lived in Kibbutzim where they worked 14 days a month as a way of life. Haim Levanon St 10, Tel. 03-643.6393, Su., Mo. + We. 09.00-17.00, Tu. 09.00-20.00, Th. 09.00-14.00 Fr. 09.00-13.00, palmach_reservation@mod.gov.il, http://info.palmach.org.il

6.1.3 Biographies

Some museums are dedicated to public figures like Chaim Bialik, Yitzhak Rabin or David Ben-Gurion. In most cases, the street is also named after them.

11.) The **Ben-Gurion House** is where Israel's first Prime Minister, David Ben-Gurion and his wife Paula lived. The house and all furniture and personal belongings are preserved as they were, including the comprehensive private library. The visitor gains insight of the public and private life of the politician. Ben-Gurion Boulevard 17, Tel. 03-522.1010, Su.-Th. 08.00-15.00, Mo. 08.00-17.00, Fr. 08.00-13.00, Sa 08.00-14.00, http://www.bg-house.org, bghouse@bezeqint.net

12) **Chaim Nachman Bialik** was one of the most celebrated among the Israeli poets and renowned for his children books. Even though the museum is almost exclusively in Hebrew (you can get a folder with English translations of the Hebrew texts at the entrance), the interior of this villa from 1925 is worth the visit: a colorful mix of different styles, very typical for its time. Bialik St. 22, Tel. 03-525.4530, Mo.-Th. 09.00-17.00, Fr. + Sa. 10.00-14.00, www.beithair.org (in Hebrew).

6.1.4 Art

Tel Aviv is rich in art, whether galleries, art museums or even in the street.

13.) The **Tel Aviv Museum of Art** is the primary point of reference for the Israeli art scene. The museum is subdivided into the main house, the Helena Rubinstein Pavilion for Contemporary Art and the spectacular Herta and Paul Amir building that was finished at the end of 2011. In addition to different collections and works of Israeli and international artists, the museum offers a wide range of activities with special exhibitions, readings, dance performances and films. Among the collections are also the famous "Miniature Rooms" by Helena Rubinstein. The Pavilion for Contemporary Art is not at the same address as the rest of the museum; it is a neighbor of the theater HaBima at the end of Rothschild Blvd. 27, Tel. 03-607.7000, Mo., We., Sa. 10.00-18.00, Tu. + Th. 10.00-21.00, Fr. 10.00-14.00, http://www.tamuseum.com, info@tamuseum.com.

14.) The **Helena Rubinstein Pavilion for Contemporary Art** is not only set apart from the rest of the museum, it also has an outstanding personality: it is a platform the Art Museum provides for young artists. Tarsat Blvd. 6, Tel. 03- 528.7196, Mo., We., Sa. 10.00-18.00, Tu. + Th. 10.00-21.00, Fr. 10.00-14.00, http://www.tamuseum.com, info@tamuseum.com

15.) The **Nachum Gutman Museum** is located in the Writer's House that used to be the seat of the newspaper "HaPoel HaZair". The museum shows many of Gutman's works which is not only a collection of extraordinary paintings; he was also famous for his prose, children's books and illustrations. His mosaic works decorate the walls of the hall in the Shalom Tower. The museum also shows works of lesser known names and of Arab Israelis as well who focus on the depiction of the Arab culture in Israeli art. Rokach St. 21, Tel. 03-516.1970, Mo.-Th. 10.00-16.00, Fr. 10.00-14.00, Sa. 10.00-15.00. http://www.gutmanmuseum.co.il/en/,

16.) The **Ilana Goor Museum** is an institution in Jaffa. The artist has spent many years in refurbishing this ruin from the 18th century for private and public use. In Ilana's atelier, no everyday item is safe from being turned into art. The museum shows paintings, sculptures and furniture from Ilana Goor and other artists. The view from the roof terrace is breathtaking. Mazal Dagim St. 4, Tel. 03-683.7676, Su.-Fr. 10.00-16.00, Sa. 10.00-18.00, before holidays 10.00-14.00. http://www.ilanagoor.org, tours@ilanagoor.org

17.) The **Rokach House** was built in 1887 by Shimon Rokach, one of the founding fathers of Neve Tzedek. His house was one the first in the new neighborhood outside Jaffa. The house had been saved from being torn down by Rokach's granddaughter, the sculptor Leah Majaro-Mintz, then refurbished and finally opened for exhibitions. Even though the documentation in the museum is entirely in Hebrew, the film about the first years of Neve Tzedek can also be seen in English. The historic photo collection is also very interesting, as much as Leah's works and the furniture from the late 19th century. Rokach St. 36, Tel. 03-516.8042, Su.-Th. 10.00-16.00, Fr., Sa. in the week of Pesach 10.00-14.00. http://rokach-house.co.il/, info@rokach-house.co.il.

18.) city of Tel Aviv and in Palestine before the founding of the State of Israel. The museum presents a permanent exhibition — often complemented with special shows, the original atelier, a room with his private belongings and a reading room. Families and children are very welcome and can participate in the workshops. The museum exhibits online the works of children who were inspired by Reuven Rubin. Bialik St. 14, Tel. 03-525.5961, Mo., We.-Fr. 10.00-15.00. Tu. 10.00-20.00, Sa. 11.00-14.00, So. geschlossen. http://www.rubinmuseum.org.il.

6.1.5 Religious Museums

19.) The **Beit Hatefutsot** (Hebrew for House of the Diaspora) is the Museum of the Jewish Diaspora. The history of the last 2,000 years of the Jews outside Israel is told on several floors. The museum is innovative and examines the subject from different angles with additional temporary exhibitions. Tel Aviv University Campus, Klausner St.; Matatia Gate 2, Tel. 3-745.7808, Su.-Tu. 10.00-16.00, We. + Th. 10.00-19.00, Fr. 09.00-13.00, http://www.bh.org.il.

!!! You can combine the visit to this museum with a free guided walk of the campus that is offered each Monday (see Guided Walks.)

6.1.6   Israeli History and Culture

There are two museums with a very similar name: the Eretz Israel Museum and the Israeli Museum; they are even on the same street. The first is an open air museum, the other one belongs to the Yitzhak Rabin Center.

20.) The **Eretz Israel Museum** is located in the north of Tel Aviv close to Yarkon Park. The museum emphasizes the diversity of the Land of Israel (Eretz Israel): archeology, botany, culture, folklore, modern life, etc. Within the park-like outdoor installation, little pavilions show different aspects. The entrance fee for the planetarium is not included in the museum ticket. Haim Levanon St. 2, Tel. 03-641-5244, Su.-We. 10.00-16.00, Th. 10.00-20.00, Fr. 10.00-14.00, Sa. 10.00-16.00. http://www.eretzmuseum.org.il

21.) Unweit des Eretz Israel Museum, the impressive architecture of the Yitzhak Rabin Center with the **Israeli Museum** inside is difficult to miss; the white roof resembles the Sydney Opera House from far away. This museum deals with modern Israeli society and the development of democracy. It exhibits political events in Israel during the lifetime of Yitzhak Rabin and gives an insight of the private person Yitzhak Rabin behind the prominent politician. The museum belongs to the Yitzhak Rabin Center which was inaugurated in November 2005, 10 years after Rabin was murdered. The center researches the effects the murder had on the Israeli society. Guided tours are available every hour, but reservations are recommended. Haim Levanon St. 14, Tel. 03-745.3313/ 19, Su., Mo., We. 09.00-17.00, Tu.+Th. 09.00-19.00, Fr. 09.00-14.00, http://www.rabincenter.org.il , Order1@rabincenter.org.il

6.1.7   Museums in Ramat Gan

Ramat Gan is the eastern neighbor of Tel Aviv. The Diamond Museum is located just inside the city border.

22.) The **Harry Oppenheimer Diamond Museum** is interesting for all ages. It is located inside the Diamond Center. International exhibits, videos, multimedia presentations and high-end temporary exhibitions show the visitor the world of the precious diamonds, about excavation methods, production and deriving products other than jewelry of which there are also nice pieces to see. .Jabotinsky St. 1, Ramat Gan, Tel. 03-576.0219, Su.-Th. 10.00-16.00, Tu. 10.00-18.00, support@israelidiamond.co.il

6.1.8 Museums in Holon

Holon is located south of Tel Aviv and very well connected by bus. From Rothschild Blvd., it is only 8 km and even a taxi is not too expensive. Bus No. 3 can be taken at the corner of Allenby and Rothschild/Lilienblum. If you do not have much time, you should definitely make sure you do not miss the Design Museum (4.)

1.) The **Israeli Center for Digital Art** is an alternative museum for video, audio and digital art in general. The exhibiting artists come from all over the world, not only Israel. HaAmoraim St. 4, Holon, Tel. 03-556.8792, Tu. + We. 16.00-20.00, Th. 10.00-14.00, Fr. + Sa. 10.00-15.00. Bus Nr. 3: stop Aharonovich/ HaTsionut. info@digitalartlab.org.il, www.digitalartlab.org.il

2.) The **Children's Museum** is a fantastic place for children aged 2-10 and their parents. The website informs about all the activities, but you have to make a reservation to participate because the activities are all moderated events. Currently, there are only activities in Hebrew and English but you should ask about your language; the museum is very creative and might offer something that suits you. In the past, the museum celebrated a success with the guided tours "Invitation to Silence" and "Dialogue in the Dark" where children learned to understand the world as a deaf or blind person.Mifrats Shlomo St. 1, Holon. Tel. 03-650.3006, Sa. 10.00-17.00, Bus Nr. 3 stop „Mifrats Shlomo/ Moshe Sharet" (close to Yamit 2000), http://www.childrensmuseum.org.il

3.) The **Cartoon Museum** is the first of its kind in Israel. The permanent exhibition is as manifold as the events with international artists who take not only Israel but the whole world in their focus of comics to show the visitor the necessity for caricature in society. The event schedule is online. Weizman St. 61, Holon, Tel. 03-652.1849, Mo., We., Fr., 10:00-13:00, Tu., Th., 17:00-20:00, Sa. 10:00-15:00, Bus Nr. 3: stop HaHistadrut/ Weizman, http://www.cartoon.org.il

4.) The new **Design Museum** is already impressive from the outside but the admiration continues inside. Constantly changing exhibitions with international artists, monthly special venues and activities for the whole family (like "Nights in the Museum") turn the museum into a very special place. Pinhas Eilon St. 8, Holon, Tel. 073-215.1515, Mo.-We. 10.00-16.00, Tu.+Th. 10.00-18.00. Fr. 10.00-14.00, Sa. 10.00-18.00, Bus Nr. 3: stop Golda Meir / Holon Kanyion (Shopping Mall). http://www.dmh.org.il,

6.2 Galleries

The ethnic and cultural plurality of Israel is also reflected in the gallery scene. It is impossible to list all galleries, there are probably around 100 in Tel Aviv. This selection contains the most renowned, established, alternative, critical, etc.,… among them.

1.) The **Center for Contemporary Art (CCA)** is by far one of the most creative spaces in Tel Aviv with a huge archive for video art with currently about 3,000 works. The CCA also offers workshops for children as well as extension studies for film artists and curators. A visit to the CCA is an absolute must if you want to get acquainted with the local scene. Kalisher 5, Tel. 03-510.6111, Mo-Th. 14:00-19:00, Fr-Sa 10:00-14:00, http://cca.org.il, info@cca.org.il

2.) A gentle breeze is going through Israel's leading pop art gallery, **Art Time Israel**. It is a very unique collection; new technology underlines the highlights. The gallery also acts as an agent for sellers. If you are interested in an estimate for your artwork from a Jewish or Israeli artist, you can send a photo by email. The Tel Aviv branch of the Jerusalem-based gallery is represented at two show rooms in the Dan Hotel. Dan Hotel, HaYarkon 87, Tel. 03-529.3548, Su.-Th. 10.00-19.00, Fr. 10.00-13.30, http://www.art-time.co.il

3.) **Dvir** is THE reference for established Israeli and international artists and those who are about to consolidate their career. The gallery participates in international art fairs (Frieze New York, Art Basel, etc.), thus the art exhibited in their own space is of top-class. Reshit Chochma 14, Tel. 03-604.3003, Tu.-Th. 11.00-18.00, Fr.-Sa. 10.00-13.00, http://www.dvirgallery.com, info@dvirgallery.com

4.) Since its founding in Neve Tzedek in 1985, the **Chelouche Gallery** has exhibited works from local and international artists and is today renowned for contemporary art. The works are extensive and of diverse characters and forms: sculptures, video art, paintings, installations, etc. In October 2010, the gallery moved to Mazeh Street, a spectacular building by Josef Berliner, the so-called "Twin House". It was the first of its kind and was supposed to be the home of the architect and his brother, but later, the Association of Architects and Engineers and the Academy for Architecture moved in. Mazeh St. 7, Tel. 03-620.0068, Mo.-Th. 11.00-19.00, Fr 10.00-14.00, Sa. 11.00-14.00, http://www.chelouchegallery.com

5.) The **Hezi Cohen Gallery** can be considered the "free spirit" among the galleries; where else in this country would it be possible to get in touch with an Iranian artist? In 2011, Iranian artist Mitra Tabrizian exhibited his work, "tension". Hezi Cohen wants to show the artworks in their self-defined nature and provides an exhibition space of 450 m² on two levels that individually adapt to the exhibits. Wolfson St. 54, Tel. 03-639.8788, Mo.-Th. 10.30-19.00, Fr. 10.00-14.00, Sa. 11.00-14.00 http://www.hezicohengallery.com, info@hezicohengallery.com

6.) The **Alfred Gallery** was founded in 2005 by a group of artists and is a true non-profit organization. Their aim is to give the not-yet-established a chance to exhibit their work. The exhibits are each of very different kinds (paintings, sculptures, photos, etc.) and are very often rotated with new ones. Simtat Shlush 5, Tel. 03-518.3313, Tu.-Th. 17.00-21.00, Fr. 10.00-14.00, Sa. 11.00-15.00, http://alfredgallery.com, alfred.hecht@gmail.com

7.) Nomen est omen, **Florentin 45** is located right here. The gallery is very dynamic and shows all the time new exhibits of modern Israeli art, much of it comes from the best ateliers Israel has to offer. 45, Florentin, Tel. 050-276.3249, Mo.–Sa. 11.00–13.00, Mo.–Th. 16.00–18.00. Florentin 45, Tel. 050-276.3249, Mo.-Sa. 11.00-13.00, We. + Th. auch 16.00-18.00, http://www.florentin45.com

8.) **Sommer Contemporary Art** was founded in 1999 by Irit Fine Sommer, who has since then not grown weary to seek those artists who have the potential for the big success of tomorrow. Her gallery lifted the local art scene to a new international level. Today her gallery is an institution, and is housed in a beautiful renovated building of the early Tel Aviv. Rothschild Blvd. 13, Tel. 3-516.6400, Mo.-Th. 10.00-18.00, Fr. 10.00-14.00, Sa. 11.00-13.00, http://www.sommergallery.com.

9.) The Tel Aviv **Artists House** belongs to the association of artists and sculptors, a non-commercial organization that takes care of the social needs of artists and dates back to 1934. With its manifold program of activities as well as monthly new exhibitions, this place is an important player in the local art scene. Al-Harizi St. 9, Tel. 03-524.6685, Mo.-Th. 10:00-13:00, 17:00-19:00, Fr. 10:00-13:00, Sa. 11:00-14:00, http://www.artisthouse.co.il, artassoc@bezeqint.net

10.) Some galleries are a bit more alternative than the others and their relationship with art is also different, like the P8 Art Gallery. They mainly exhibit the works of the five founders, but they also invite others artists to their space. The successful concept has led the group to leave the original space at Poriya St. 8. With the change of location, they aim to establish themselves further on the art market. Yehuda HaLevi St. 79, Tel. 050-554.3485, Tu. 11.00-13.00, We.+Th. 15.00-19.00, Fr.+Sa. 11.00-15.00. http://www.p8gallery.net, gallery.p8@gmail.com

11.) **Kibbutz, The Gallery** focuses on Israeli culture in art. The works reflect the topics of Israeli society and is connected to 15 other galleries in the kibbutzim. 25, Dov Hoz 25, Tel. 03-523.2533, Mo.-Th. 11.00-15.00, 16.00-18.00, Fr. 11.00-14.00. http://www.kibbutzgallery.org.il, kgallery@actcom.net.il.

6.3   Theaters and Concert Halls

Tel Aviv has much to offer, even for those who do not speak Hebrew because many performances come with English supertitles, e.g., at the opera. Ballet and contemporary dance are very much worth the visit as well; often these are Israeli productions.

6.3.1   Opera and Theater

1.) Tel Aviv is proud of its **opera** tradition which dates back to the 1920. Jewish-Russian composer Mordechai Golinkin dedicated his life to the creation of an opera for the Land of Israel. He most probably could have not imagined how much the Israelis would still love opera in the 21st century when he published his thesis, "The Vision of the Hebrew Art Temple of Opera Work in Palestine" in 1917.

Golinkin immigrated in 1923. On 28 July 1923, the "Palestine Opera" was born with the performance of Verdi's "La Traviata". On the way to today's "New Israeli Opera," mainly financial difficulties put the project at risk more than once, but political turbulence also put obstacles along the way. Legend has it that the British Mandate government had asked Golinkin to not show the opera "La Juive" (the Jewess) from HaLevy. The performance had already been very successful in Tel Aviv and was supposed to be shown in Jerusalem, but the British feared problems with the non-Jewish population here: Christians. Golinkin agreed but did not stop the project; he simply changed the title to "Rachel" which was the name of the main figure and performed the opera as scheduled. There are no reports about any negative reactions from the Christians.

Golinkin managed his opera house until 1927 when he left for the US to raise funds. Later, in 1940, George Singer and Riga-born Marc Lavry founded the "Palestine Folk Opera." Lavry had been the manager of the Berlin Symphony Orchestra between 1929 and 1932, and in the following two years, the opera in Riga. In 1935, he fled to Israel. His opera production "Dan HaShomer" (Dan the Watchman) was shown in Tel Aviv in 1945. It was the first opera production in the country and was based on a play from Shin Shalom. It became Lavry's very own signature to reflect political events in his work, especially topics referring to the European presence in the Near East and the conflicts with the Arab population.

Edis de Philippe (*1912, New York) is another name that is deeply connected with the Israeli opera culture. Singer de Philippe successfully convinced the Zionist Union in Basel that Tel Aviv needed a permanent and locally based opera. From 1947 until her death in 1979, she directed the "National Israeli Opera". Under her auspices, many Israeli but also international singers started their careers, like Plácido

Domingo who studied here in the 1960s.

Until 1958, de Philippe was renting space from local theaters and would then move to 1, Allenby Street, the former seat of parliament. In the early years, de Philippe funded the opera house with her own money, but in 1982, it was finally closed due to lack of funding; neither the state nor the municipality was willing to give more grants. De Philippe had been a controversial figure, many would even call her management a dictatorship. She had dedicated her life to the Israeli opera culture and thanks to her, the citizens of Tel Aviv never lost their enthusiasm for it.

It is no wonder that in the years following the closure, they would express their displeasure about this loss. Finally, the New Israeli Opera was founded. It is a joint-venture between the Cameri Theater and the Israeli Chamber Orchestra which is located in the Tel Aviv Performing Art Center (TAPAC) with 1,500 seats since 1994. The operas are sung in the original language with Hebrew and English supertitles.

Guided tours (by reservation):
For groups, there is the so-called Backstage Tour in English (and Hebrew). In a 90-minute guided tour, you can look behind the scenes. The price is about 30 NIS. Tel Aviv Performing Arts Center, Shaul Ha Melech Blvd. 19, box office: kupa@tapac.org.il, Tel. 03-692.7777, http://www.israel-opera.co.il

2.) Every year, more than 900,000 visitors come to the **Cameri Theater** in the TAPAC. Since its founding in 1944, it is an inherent part of Israeli culture. The Cameri wants to give more than a good performance; it wants to bring the theater to everybody. It is a theater with social responsibility: translations into different languages, special tariffs, barrier-free, etc. Three times a week, the Cameri plays with English supertitles: "See it in Hebrew read it in English". Tel Aviv Performing Arts Center, Shaul Ha Melech Blvd. 19, Tel. 03- 03-606.1900, http://www.cameri.co.il

3.) **HaBima** is Israel's national theater. It was founded already in 1913 in Russia and had always struggled with anti-Semitic hostility until the 1920s when the group decided to split during a concert tour in the United States. HaBima started again in 1931 in Tel Aviv and moved into its own theater house in 1945 even before the construction was finished. Since HaBima had been awarded the Israel Prize (that acknowledges engagement for Israeli society) in 1958, the Israelis call it THE Israeli theater house. It is the only member of the European Theater Union (UTE) outside Europe and performs around the globe. Information on performances in English: on request. Kikar HaBima, Tel. 03-629.5555, sherut@habima.org.il, http://www.habima.co.il.

4.) The **Yiddish Theatre** in Israel is one of the most charming among all theaters. As the name already indicates, they play in Yiddish. Headphones with simultaneous translations are provided only in Hebrew and Russian. The company published some examples of its repertoire on YouTube. This way, you can test whether you understand the Yiddish language. The actors are fabulous. They show Jewish culture from many angles, whether traditional, eastern European or modern productions, the Yiddish Theatre hits the mark. The group performs all over the country; in Tel Aviv they are located at the Arison Auditorium for the Arts (4a). Sa'adia Gaon St. 7, box office Carlebach St. 7, (4b), Tel. 03-525.4660, open Su.-Th. 09.00-20.00, Fr. 09.00-13.00.
http://www.youtube.com/user/yiddishpiel, http://www.yiddishpiel.co.il,

5.) A visit to the **Na Laga'at Center** in Jaffa port is a very enriching experience. While Israeli shops often put little signs on their goods with "na lo laga'at" ("please do not touch,") here, we are in a "please touch" space. Blind and deaf actors present an impressive show with English supertitles on Sunday, Tuesday and Thursday at 20.30 (subject to change!) In the center, there is also the Kapish Café and the Black Out Restaurant, a dark restaurant with blind waiters. Rezif HaAliya HaShniya, Jaffa Port, Tel. 03-633.0808, http://www.nalagaat.org.il, theater1@nalagaat.org.il, http://www.youtube.com/user/nalagaat

6.) **Mayúmana** is an international creative group that communicates with the audience in its very own way. The participants are actors, musicians, dancers, acrobats in one. Lots of rhythm and visual effects flow from the stage into the audience. Founded by three Israelis, Mayumana has become so successful that they decided to have two groups: one performs in Tel Aviv and another one is always on tour. Mayúmana House, Louis Pasteur St. 15, Tel. 03-681.1787, www.mayumana.com, www.youtube.com/user/mayumanamomentum, info@mayumana.com

7.) The **Clipa Theater**, founded in 1995, is considered Israel's best "visual theater" Idit Herman and Dmitry Tyulpanov have founded a company that combines contemporary dance and musical effects in a new way and with self-designed costumes. HaRakevet St. 38, Tel. 03-639.9090, info@clipa.co.il, www.youtube.com/user/clipatheater, http://www.clipa.co.il

6.3.2 Classical Music

8.) The Israeli Philharmonic Orchestra (IPO), originally "The Palestine Symphony", is world-renowned and looks back on 75 years of history. On 26 December 1936, the IPO gave its first concert directed by conductor Arturo Toscanini on the fairgrounds in the north of Tel Aviv. Prior to this, the Polish violinist Bronisław Huberman (1882–1947) had convinced 75 Jewish colleagues from different European countries to immigrate to Palestine to found a new orchestra. Huberman saw no future for Jewish musicians in fascist Europe where more and more of them were harassed and became jobless. In the first two years, the orchestra would still play many works from Richard Wagner, a known anti-Semite, but since the "Night of the Broken Glass" ("Reichskristallnacht") of 9 November 1938, the orchestra adheres to its ban of Wagner compositions. 1936 was also the year of birth of the Indian conductor Zubin Mehta who was appointed music director for life of the orchestra. Since 1968, he had already been their advisor. Leonard Bernstein (1918-1990) was another big name that collaborated with the orchestra since 1948, and who in 1988 became awarded with the title of "conductor of honor" of the orchestra. Bernstein and Mehta are, of course, extraordinary musicians, but there is one other reason why the Israelis love them dearly: both never left the country during wars. They organized concerts at war places to morally support the population and the soldiers. Since 1957, the Frederic R. Mann Auditorium at the upper end of Rothschild Boulevard is the permanent home of the orchestra, right next to HaBima Theater. The building was financially supported from the American philanthropist Frederic R. Mann (1904-1987) from Philadelphia, an international promoter of art and music projects. Frederic R. Mann Auditorium, Huberman St. 1, Tel. 03-621.1777, http://www.youtube.com/user/IPOvideos, http://www.ipo.co.il

9.) Together with the IPO, the **Israeli Chamber Orchestra (ICO)** belongs to the most renowned in Israel. It was founded in 1965 by Gary Bertini, an Israeli conductor and composer. The ICO plays music from Israeli and international composers, contemporary as well as baroque. The participation of the ICO at the Wagner festivals in Bayreuth, Germany, in 2011 was discussed very controversially. They were the first Israeli orchestra to play Wagner, unlike the IPO which refused to play Wagner since 1938. Israel Chamber Orchestra, She'erit Israel St. 10, Tel. 03-518.8845-0, Tel. Tickets 03-518.8845-5, http://www.ico.co.il

10.) The youngest of the local orchestras is the **Israeli Contemporary Players (ICP)**. Founded in 1991, the orchestra plays mainly music from the 20th century, often from Israeli composers. The musicians perform at different venues throughout the city; many of their events take place in the Recanati Hall of the Tel Aviv Museum of Art. http://www.ensemble21.org.il.

11.) The Felicja Blumental Music Center is home to an extensive music library since 1951 and frequently organizes concerts, workshops and further education. The house is idyllically located next to Tel Aviv's first city hall at the end of Bialik St. In 1991, the center was named after Polish born pianist Felicja Blumental (1908-1991.) Since 1999, the Felicja Blumental Festival takes place every year (April/ May), organized from the Tel Aviv Museum of Art. Every day, there are up to 5 events filled with theater plays, music and films in different venues in the city. Bialik St. 26, Tel. 03-620.1185, info@fbmc.co.il, www.fbmc.co.il, www.blumentalfestival.com.

12.) **Tzafta** is a little theater that also offers classical concerts every Saturday at 11.11 am. Ibn Gvirol St. 30, Tel. 03-695.0156/7; opening hours box office: Su.-Th. 10.00-16.00 & 19.00-20.30, Fr: 10.00-14.00 & 19.00-01.00, Sa: 10.00-11.30 & 19.00-21.00, keren@tzavta.co.il, http://www.tzavta.co.il (Hebrew)

13.) The Tel Aviv Museum of Art houses the **Recanati Hall**. Handpicked concert series, contemporary art performances and a high-quality standard turn the hall into a very sought after venue. Shaul Hamelech Blvd. 27, Tel. 03-607.7009, music@tamuseum.com, http://www.tamuseum.com/music-lobby

6.3.3 Dance

14.) The Suzanne Dellal Center is all about dance: education, training, workshops, festivals. Founded in 1989, the center is situated in a palace-like residence in the heart of Neve Tzedek and shows more than 750 events every year. Three stages and the box office are located at the site. Pre-purchased tickets can be returned up to 48 hours before the performance and a full refund will be issued. Yechieli St. 5, Tel. 03-510.5657, info@suzannedellal.org.il, box office: Tel. 03-510.5656, Su.-Th. 09.00-19:00, Fr and before holidays 09.00-13.00, as well as 2 hours before start of show, www.suzannedellal.org.il, www.youtube.com/user/suzannedellalcentre

6.3.4   Culture - Miscellaneous

Foreign Cultural Representations
Many foreign institutions offer a very interesting cultural program and are very open to tourists and non-Hebrew speakers. Please consult their websites for further information.

15.) **Goethe Institut**, Asia House, Weizmann St. 4, Tel. 03-606.0500, info@telaviv.goethe.org, http://www.goethe.de/telaviv (German, Hebrew)

16.) **Instytut Polski**, Asia House, Weizmann St. 4, Tel. 03-696.2053/9, telaviv@instytutpolski.org, http://www.polishinstitute.org.il (Polish, English, Hebrew),

17.) **Czech Centre**, Zeitlin St. 23, Tel. 03-691.1216, cctelaviv@czech.cz, http://tel-aviv.czechcentres.cz (Czech, English).

18.) **Romanian Culture Institute**, Shaul Ha Melech 8, Tel. 03-696.1746, office@icrtelaviv.org, http://www.icr.ro/tel-aviv (Romanian, Englisch).

19.) **Instituto Cervantes**, Shulamit St. 7, Tel. 03-527.9992, centel@cervantes.es, http://telaviv.cervantes.es (Spanish, Hebrew).

20.) **L' Institut Français**, Rothschild Blvd. 7, Tel. 03-796.8000, http://institutfrancais-israel.com/blog/tel-aviv (French, Hebrew), accueilifta@ambfr-il.org.

21.) **Instituto Italiano di Cultura**, HaMered 25, Tel. 03-516.1361, http://www.iictelaviv.esteri.it/IIC_Telaviv (Italian, Hebrew), iictelaviv@esteri.it.

6.3.5   Tickets
Most of the local event tickets can be purchased at

22.) Le'an, Dizengoff St. 101 Tel: 03-524.7373

7 Eating Out

Tel Aviv's restaurants are among the most creative and exotic in the world. This special fusion of Jewish traditional food influenced by the immigrants' home countries like Poland, Russia, Morocco, Persia, etc., created a totally new cuisine of "Ethno Food," spiced with the Near East flavor. It is nearly impossible to not eat well in Israel. Even the cocktail bars offer more than just snacks. Every restaurant offers a lunch menu and in the upper class restaurants, these are real bargains in comparison to the prices in the evening. Tip is about 15%.

Israelis eat more than they drink and there is practically no bar that does not cater some snacks. Most bars call themselves resto-bars and what they offer is actually more than a simple snack– even at a late hour. While restaurants tend to describe the food on the menu, the street food is for the savvy. Here is some gastro-vocabulary:

Sabih
is served in pita bread that is filled with mashed and fried eggplants, sesame cream, a boiled egg, salad etc., as you like. Ever since sabih was introduced to the local food market by Iraqi Jews, nobody wants to miss it.

Falafel
is also served in pita bread but instead of the eggplant, the falafel contains fried balls from chickpeas and/or fava beans, sesame cream and pickles as well as tomatoes, onions, etc., add what you like.

Shavarma
comes in different varieties depending on the type of meat and dressing. The thin meat layers are stuffed into the pita bread and the other ingredients are similar to sabih and falafel, and if you want, you can even add some fries on top.

Laffa
is a large, round, thin bread that is baked on a special curved plate, called Tabun. When finished, it is rolled up together with meat, lettuce, pickles, etc. It is a quite filling meal.

Humus

is made from mashed chickpeas and tahini, lemon juice and olive oil are added as well as garlic and salt. It is served with pita bread. Every Israeli has his/her favorite Hummus shop; in Tel Aviv, most are located in the south.

Shakshuka

is a pan dish mixing fresh tomatoes, herbs, onions, sometimes also chili before eggs are finally added. Originally from Northern Africa, Shakshuka has become the Israeli national dish. Most hotels have it on their buffet.

Jachnun

is a gift of the Yemeni cuisine. The thin sweet sheets of dough are rolled up and cooked for 10 hours. They are eaten with an egg and hot sauce.

Where to eat?

Of course, this depends. The longer you live in Tel Aviv, the more you will become an expert yourself. The following places attract a large audience with what they have to offer:

Sabich and Falafel

1.) Shlomo & Sons
has been located directly on the green center strip of Sderot Nordau / corner Ben Yehuda for over 40 years. It is one of the best falafel places in town. They also make fresh salads, omelettes and Shakshuka.

2.) Sabich Frishman. You cannot miss it: right on the corner of Frishman and Dizengoff Street you will see a long line of people waiting for their food

Humus

Everybody claims to know the best Hummus place. The traditional shops open in the morning and once the fresh Hummus is sold, they close again, normally in the early evening, or even before.

3.) **Abu Hassan** (Ajami) is a classic. Abu Hassan has been around for ages and can be considered a landmark. The place opens at 8.00 in the morning and by 15.00 is already closed again, all the hummus is sold. You can dine in or take it home. 1, HaDolfin St. Ajami, border with Jaffa.

4**.) Abu Dubby** (center north) offers Hummus with Jamaica flavor. You may enjoy your hummus together with reggae music, even on Shabbat. 81, King George St. 81/ Bar Giora.

Shakshuka

You will find it on nearly every menu, and in your hotel buffet even in the morning. But one restaurant you must not miss:

5.) "**Dr. Shakshuka**". You can either go to the uncrowned shakshuka king from Tripoli (3, Beit Eshel St. near Clock Tower), or you can try a more home-made variant as it is eaten in many Israeli homes every day: Shlomo & Sons (Nr. 1).

Is all that kosher?
Tel Aviv is a very secular city and not all restaurants are kosher (in Hebrew: ka-shér, meaning: suitable), but many are. If you are still wondering why there is no cheese on the salami pizza or why that cheese is artificial, here is a little introduction to the Jewish dietary laws, called kashrut (speak: kash-root)

What is kashrut?
Kashrut is dietary law. It prescribes which foods maybe eaten at all, especially which animals (see 3rd book of Moses.) It is not allowed to consume blood, and meat and dairy have to be strictly separated from each other (no cheese burger, no cordon bleu allowed.) Neutral foods are "parve", meaning not dairy, not meat, e.g., vegetables and fruits. Cheese is a difficult product since it is made with the help of ab-ferment, traditionally coming from animals, but nowadays it is possible to make hard cheese from microbial lab-ferment.

How do I know whether it is kosher?
Kosher food is labeled as are restaurants. The label can also be found on products

that are naturally kosher like wine, but where the production in an un-kosher factory could add impurities. The label is supervised by the rabbinate. In the US, you often find on the products the letter "U" from the Orthodox Union. In other countries, it might look like a stamp and shows the name of the certifier.

7.1 Coffee & Cafés

Israelis love coffee and dispute with Spaniards and Italians who makes the best. The big Israeli coffee shop chain AROMA CAFÉ (black logo, white and red letters) offers not only hot drinks and cakes but also salads and sandwiches. At the port (nemal) of Tel Aviv, you will find a couple of cafés next to the water where you can sit down on the big wooden step and enjoy a coffee or while contemplating the sea.

Do you drink your coffee with milk? You might want to try an "upside-down coffee," called coffee afuch, where the milk sits on top of the coffee. In summer, you will find many cafés offering "coffee barad," in Europe called frappé, with crushed ice. The Israelis have a product even for the lovers of Turkish coffee: the "mud coffee", coffee botz. Turkish coffee is put together with sugar into the cup and hot water added.

6.) Founded in 1919 by Moshe Landwer from Berlin, Landwer was Israel's first coffee brand. The **Café Landwer** is an old classic in Tel Aviv. It has become a chain with several venues in the city. One of the nicest can be found in the Gan Meir Park (Rabenu Tam St. 7) This little oasis seems to be far away from the buzzing city and invites you to stay for a coffee and some cake or sandwich, or soup, or… . Another nice Landwer Café is the one at the marina (Eliezer Peri St. 14). Recently the chain opened a café in the new shopping village of Sarona (Osvaldo Aranha St. 13). Landwer is open daily from 08.00-00.00.

7.) **Dallal** is not only an exquisite restaurant, they also have an excellent bakery-café close by (Kol Israel Haverim 7) Mousses, éclairs, tarts, quiches… the most exquisite pastries lie at your feet. A great place to have a coffee in the center of Neve Tzedek.Su.-Th. 07.00-22.00, Fr. 07.00-17.00.

8.) **Max Brenner** (45, Rothschild Blvd. and Yarkon estuary in the port) is the name of Tel Aviv's chocolate planet. Chocolate in all varieties (to eat, to drink, hot, cold, spiced, black, white…) can be found on the menu and in the shop. Max Brenner also offers a creative selection of sandwiches, pasta, entrecotes and salads. http://www.maxbrenner.com

9.) The port of Jaffa is the home of the **Café Kapish** which is part of the Na Laga'at Center (see Theaters.) Open every day from 09.00 to 23.00, Fridays until 16.00 and closed on shabbat. The café offers not only a great Israeli breakfast in a place a bit off the beaten path but also amazing cocktails (try the apple-jito or kir royal with pomegranate.) The highlights of the menu are the cheese cake with strawberry sauce, the pasta the hummus and great Israeli breakfast.

10.) The **Delicatessen Tel Aviv** (Yehuda HaLevi St. 79/81) appears very European, a mix of restaurant, bakery and a French bistro. It is a great place for a snack, lunch or a light early dinner. .And it is open on shabbat! Su.-Th. 07.30-20.00, Fr. until 17.00, Sa. 08.00-17.00. Tel. 03-968.1010.

7.2 Restaurants

The Israeli dress code is rather casual, but always cool. This is important. Nobody will turn you away only because you are wearing jeans or the wrong label. Even outdoor sandals are not a general no-go, but: the better the restaurant, the less people are willing to see outdoor.

Even though you can pay with credit card in nearly all places, little neighborhood eateries will not likely accept them. Here are some recommendations to have the ultimate local gourmet experience:

Yemenite

The following selected Yemenite restaurants are little family eateries around the Carmel Market where the neighborhood has lunch at reasonable prices. In the little streets around the market, you will discover even more. The tasty food is served with bread and spicy sauces (skhug.) Having lunch here will make you feel like a local. Between 12.00 and 13.30, the places are very full and you might have to wait a bit for a table.

1.) **Eres**, Nahliel St. 24, Tel. 03-510.2555
Great quality for little money. Probably one of the best shnitzels in town.

2.) **Rina & Zacharia**, HaKovshim St. 22
Their soups are legendary and the house specializes in typical Yemenite food with a variety of meat.

Oriental

3.) **Odelia** (Ben Yehuda St 89) is a reasonably priced restaurant where you can travel culinarily through the Near East: rice, lamb, vegetables, couscous, hummus.... Tel. 03-681.8793.

4.) **Maganda** (Rabbi Meir St. 26) is a small kosher restaurant with a very long tradition. It is located at the same place since its founding back in 1927. The restaurant is richly decorated with historic photos and newspaper clippings. The kitchen is a journey through the Middle East. They also offer excellent wines from the Golan Heights. Tel. 03-517-9990

Fusion/ Mediterranean
The Jewish immigration from different countries has left its mark on the loca

cuisine and over the years, the chefs have created dishes nobody wants to miss.

5.) **Claro** (Rav Aluf David Elazar St. 30) belongs to the famous Israeli chef Ran Shmueli and is a new star on Tel Aviv's gourmet sky. Houses in a historic Templar building, the restaurant offers mediterranean kitchen with Israeli flavor. Tel. 3-6017.777

6.) **Cheder Ha Ochel** means "dining room" (23, Shaul Ha Melech Blvd.) and is located at the Tel Aviv Performing Art Center (TAPAC.) Have a seat at the long tables and enjoy the company. The restaurant presents itself in a very modest style and focuses on the food which comes like tapas in little portions. Due its proximity to the opera, this place is very full shortly before and after the performance. Tel. 03-696.6188.

7.) The name **Coffee Bar** (13, Haruzim St.) is a discreet understatement for a restaurant in the budgetary upper middle class. Located since 1994 in an area where not many go for a stroll, the Coffee Bar has become one of the best restaurants in town. It is open 7 days a week; breakfast is served from 09.00-12.00, except on Shabbat when a special family lunch is offered. From Sunday to Thursday, they offer a business lunch from 12.00-17.00, the dinner follows on seamlessly, Tel. 03-688.9696, http://www.coffeebar.co.il

Outside

8.) Neve Tzedek without *Susanna* (8, Shabazi St.)? Impossible! In the heart of Neve Tzedek, a beautiful terrace offers a shady refuge on those hot days. Whether you are simply looking for a nice cup of good coffee or a large dinner, Susanna's kitchen is delicious and also suitable for vegetarians! In summer they open the roof terrace. With a drink in your hand, you can now enjoy the village flair of this beautiful old neighborhood. Tel. 03-517.7580.

9.) Das **Bellini** (Yechieli St. 6) is located close to the Suzanne Dellal Center. A nice Italian family restaurant on a quiet side street with a shady terrace. Open every day from 12.00 to midnight, the Bellini offers a very good menu with renowned Italian food and dishes from "la mamma." Every day, there is a different lunch special or you can eat à la carte. The main dishes start around 65 NIS. Tel. 057-943.9619, http://www.bellini.co.il.

10.) **Vicky Cristina** is a tapas bar and restaurant in the old train station HaTachana. The wine bar curls around the big old tree and the guests enjoy Spanish rhythm, beautiful decor, food (from Vicky) and wine (from Cristina) as if they were in Spain. Wine is their specialty; the list contains 120 different names. Tel. 03-736.7272.

Jewish / Eastern European

11.) Since 1948, **Monka** (Yehuda St. HaYamit 15) serves Bulgarian specialties such as tarator soup (cold cucumber soup) and offal (ox testis, lung, etc.). The kitchen is so rich and diverse that even vegetarians can enjoy a meal at Monka's; fresh salads and home-made bread are part of the daily menu. Tel. 03-682.0707

12.) **Little Prague** (Allenby St. 56), is more a pub than a restaurant but also offers typical Czech food like goulash, shnitzel, cake with lemon icing, etc., and, of course, many Czech beers. Tel. 03- 516.8137. walnut

13.) **Kiton** (Dizengoff St. 145) opened in the 1940s and legend has it that the menu is still the same: kugel (sweet noodle gratins), fish, soups…, well-proven typical East-European, Jewish cuisine. Tel. 03-523.3679.

Vegetarian / Vegan

14.) **Nanuchka** (30, Lilienblum St.) is a legendary Georgian restaurant with a special flair: nice furniture, fresh flowers and old porcelain with flower design. The guests quickly feel at home and at the end of the evening, most have made new friends or dance on the bar. The later the hour, the better the party. The kitchen is very creative: when local ingredients meet Georgian tradition, the result is amazing. Main dishes start at about 55 NIS and the lunch menu at 49 NIS. In 2014, the restaurant decided to become vegan. Tel. 03-516.2254

15.) **Budda Burgers** (21, Yehuda Ha Levi St. or 86, Ibn Gvirol St.) makes health junkies happy: for every dish, you can consult the nutrition facts and ingredients. The menu is very international: burritos, tortilla rolls, sushi, salad, soups, pasta, cakes, etc. Main courses start at 25 NIS. BB is closed on Shabbat. http://www.buddhaburgers.co.il

Gluten-free

16.) **Mezze** (51, Achad Ha'am St.) is God-sent for all those who (have to) eat gluten-free. Even though it is a general vegetarian restaurant, it offers at least one main dish (start at 40 NIS) and several desserts that are gluten-free. Open daily from 08.00-24.00, Fridays only until 17.30, closed on Shabbat. Tel. 03-629.9753., http://www.mezze.co.il/

Meat

Most Tel Aviv restaurants offer a very good meat quality, but some of them should not be missed by carnivores:

17.) Nomen est omen, **Makom Shel Basar** means "Place of Meat" (Shabazi St. 64) and here they demand a great deal of their own meat production. The restaurant has its own rooms and equipment for meat hanging and additional processing. The excellent wine selection makes the menu perfect. Makom Shel Basar is located close to Rothschild Blvd. where Neve Tzedek starts. Guests can also enjoy their meal on a very nice terrace. Meat dishes start at 130 NIS. Tel. 03-510.4021

18.) **Rak Basar** – "Only Meat" (Derech Shlomo 19) is the motto of this meat restaurant and this is the understatement of the century! Eating at Rak Basar is a great experience. Like in a butcher's shop, the guest can choose the piece with the help from an expert. Like in Makom Shel Basar, the meat is produced in-house and sold by weight. Tel. 03-681.3590.

Beach

19.) **Manta Ray** is the restaurant with the "killer location" as critics call it: Alma Beach between Charles Clore Park and Etzel Museum. The prices are still very reasonable for such an excellent oriental restaurant (main dishes start at 90 NIS.) The Manta Ray considers itself a fish restaurant but they also serve good entrecote and even vegetarian dishes. Every day from 09.00 to 12.00, you can enjoy a wonderful breakfast with pancakes, omelet, fruit, champagne… and beach! In the afternoons, you can enjoy the beach and later, the sunset with coffee and an amazing dessert (e.g., caramelized figs) and a good drink. Tel. Tel. 03-516.6516, mantaray@netvision.net.il, http://www.mantaray.co.il

Exquisite

21.) **Mul Yam** means "across the sea" (Hangar 24, Tel Aviv port.) It is the best fish restaurant in the whole of Israel and, therefore, the only Israeli restaurant that is listed in the gourmet guide "Les Tables du Monde", and deservedly so. Do not forget to order a Fabergé Egg! Business lunch is served every day – even Sundays and holidays – for 160 NIS and175 NIS respectively. In the evening, they open at

19.30, the main courses start at about 200 NIS. Tel. 03-546.9920, http://www.mulyam.com

22.) **Catit** (Nachalat Binyamin, 57) is one of the most exclusive places in town. Chef Meir Adon turns even the simplest of dishes into a gourmet meal, whether it is a Spanish almond gazpacho or sushi. Tel. 03-510.7001, catit2006@gmail.com, http://www.catit.co.il

23.) **Messa** (HaArba'a St. 19) is the stylish restaurant of chef Aviv Moshe. His specialty is the Nouvelle French Cuisine with creations like a caramelized fish with tempura avocado and lychee jelly. Main dishes start at 100 NIS. You need to reserve your table 2 days in advance! Open daily from 12.00-15.30 and 19.00-24.00. Tel. 03-685.6859, messa@messa.co.il

24.) **Dallal** (10, Shabazi St.) travels back with you into the time when Neve Tzedek was a place for Jewish entrepreneurs who had decided to leave the then-claustrophobic and crowded Jaffa to build their new homes here. This romantic restaurant was built on the ruins of three old houses, with an intimate courtyard and open air bar. The menu is well balanced between fish and meat dishes and an additional dish of the day. The prices are still reasonable: breakfast 55 NIS, main courses start at 80 NIS and the "Executive Lunch" is offered for 70-110 NIS. Tel. 03-510.9292. dallal@dallal.info, http://www.dallal.info

Breakfast

Israelis appreciate a good breakfast and nearly all restaurants start the day latest at 09.00 with a breakfast menu, whether it is the Manta Ray or the Café Landwer, they are all prepared for hungry early morning guests. The restaurant Dellal has even its own bakery and café, but the most renowned place for breakfast is Benedict.

25.) **Benedict** – "All about breakfast" (29, Rothschild Blvd.), their slogan says it all. Benedict serves breakfast 24/7: pancakes, champagne, orange juice, croissants, eggs … the perfect start to the day! Tel. 03-686.8657, http://www.benedict.co.il

8 Nightlife

Tel Aviv calls itself "the city that never stops" and this is not the whole story. Tel Aviv never stops and keeps changing within seconds; a permanent balancing act between Near Eastern lifestyle and European roots. "Being cool" is the most important task; "tradition" nearly an offense. Bars, clubs and restaurants come and go; the city shows a new face in every moment. Just one thing never changes: the late hour. Before 23.00, nothing is really going on and this is still early.

Wednesday is the best day to make sure you meet more locals than tourists. Sunday is the first work day of the week and everything is just one day earlier. Meaning: Thursday and Fridays are really full and Saturday, Shabbat, is quieter because everybody has to go back to work the next day.

Smoking
Smoking in public is quite restricted also in Israel nowadays. Since 2007, bars and restaurants have to offer non-smoking areas or they will be fined. But Tel Aviv is very generous and controls are much more relaxed than in the rest of the country; a national commission rebuked the municipality in September 2011 for its lax attitude. Rule of thumb: before you light your cigarette, have a look around what the others are doing; if controls are being imposed, both the bar owner and the smoking customer pay a fine.

Beverages
If you want to get a taste of the local lifestyle, why not order an arrak-grapefruit long drink? Tel Aviv summers are hot and a cool beer, whether Maccabi or Goldstar, is always welcome. In recent years, the wines from the Golan Heights have gained presence and have also been internationally awarded.

Israelis do not drink much really. The high number of tourists and immigrants from countries with different drinking habits have changed the bar scene in recent years. For some time now, there have been so-called "bracelet bars". In these bars, you pay a fixed price, get a wristband and thus a flat rate of alcohol.

8.1 Bars

Tel Aviv's nightlife is abundant and it is very difficult to make a decision about where to go. Sometimes, it feels like there is a new bar opening every day. If you are new in town, you can start with bar hopping around Lilienblum Street and from there explore Florentin. In the hot summers, the Tel Aviv port invites you to have a cool beer or sophisticated drink in one of the many open air bars. Dizengoff and Ibn Gvirol are also good for a decent pub crawl. You don't have to be an insider to enjoy a night out in Tel Aviv.

Beachfront

1.) **Shalvata** is a great location to start the evening or to stay all night. Centrally located in the Tel Aviv port, this place is often very crowded. Come early for an aperitif, have dinner, then go to the bar to enjoy a good drink, all while having a sea view and good music. Tel. 03-544.1279, http://www.shalvata.co.il/

2.) The **Carlton Hotel** (10, Eliezer Peri St., Hilton Beach) offers a superb refuge for hot summer evenings: from their beach bar, the guests will have a nice view of the marina; the ambiance is classy and stylish paired with perfect service and ambitious cocktails

3.) **LaLa Land** (Herbert Samuel St. 131, Gordon Beach) is a typical beach bar and cannot be missed. At any time of day, LaLa Land provides the ultimate holiday feeling: feet in the sand, drinks, sea view. The kitchen serves good hummus, typical Israeli snacks and a memorable chocolate cake. Tel. 03- 529.3303

North
4.) **223** (223, Dizengoff St./ Basel St.) is one of the coolest bars of its kind. The cocktail design is so smart that you might hesitate to drink them. The bar was founded by six local bar tenders and the result is very worthwhile seeing.Tel. 03-544.6537, info@223.co.il, http://223tlv.com

5.) **HaNevi'im** (Yeremiahu St. 54) means "the prophets" and what is prophesied to you here, is good drinks, good food and great atmosphere. The crowd is young (25-35), local and likes to dance to Israeli as well as mainstream music. Daily from 20.00. Those who would like something to eat and drink in peace should come before 22:00, for the place gets full quickly.

Center

6.) The **Meat Bar Next Door** (Chen Blvd. 52) belongs to the renowned meat restaurant "Meat Bar". It is not a restaurant but does offer very good food to the not so hungry. The kitchen prepares great roast beef sandwiches, and the bar offers an excellent choice of wines. It opens daily at 18.00. Tel. 03-695.6276.

7.) **Abraxas** (Lilienblum St. 40) is one of the most popular bars on the party mile of Lilienblum Street. Much has been written and said about Abraxas; fact is: it is still there. The snacks are good, the bar too, the guests are even more beautiful and the DJs make you dance. No particular dress code. Tel. 03-510.4435, abraxasbartlv@gmail.com, http://www.abraxas.co.il (Hebrew)

8.) **Lima Lima** (42, Lilienblum St.) is much bigger than it looks from outside. It is a mainstream bar and discotheque that reflects the flavor of the moment. The place is open every day, Monday is "Gay Night." Tel. 03-560.0924

9.) **Evita** (Yavne St. 31) claims to be the city's oldest gay bar. Everybody is welcome whether straight, gay, lesbian, bi or transsexual. Their "Eurovision Sundays" are just about the limit! Tel. 03-566.9559, http://www.evita.co.il/

10.) The **Bar Par Derriere** (King George St. 4) is a wine bar near the Carmel Market. It's an intimate oasis where you would never expect it, in a backyard of King George Street. The terrace is very romantic; life concerts turn it at the same time into an animated venue. In Tel Aviv, this bar is still a secret! Tel. 03-629.2111

South

12.) **Jajo** (Shabazi St. 44) is an intimate bar in the heart of Neve Tzedek. Surrounded by modest background music, the guests easily fall in love with the excellent wine list. Daily from 19.00, Fridays from 13.00-20.00. Tel. 03-516.4557

13.) **Bugsy** (Florentine St. 26) has already been here now for several years, which is quite an achievement in Tel Aviv. The guests love the combination of modernity, good food, moderate prices and sophisticated drinks (they have 14 different vodkas!) Maybe try it first for breakfast: wonderful pancakes with maple syrup (or maybe rather shakshuka?). Opens daily at 09.00, Shabbat at 10.00.Tel. 03 681.3138.

14.) **Perla** (Florentin St. 8)
s a lovely bar, with the typical audience from the alternative Florentin. Champions League, bachelor party, girls night out, half dim lighting, mainstream loud music,

100 different whiskeys and great atmosphere, ... this is Perla! Tel. 03-682.3823.

Jaffa

15.) **Container** (Warehouse 2) is located in the Jaffa port right next to the fishermen's boats. It is a restaurant, bar and art space in one with different DJs. Tables with white tablecloth and blue wooden chairs fit perfectly in the old port. The bar is made out of a real container, currently the "place to be." Tel. 03-683.6321.
http://www.container.org.il

16.) **Shafa Bar** (Rabbi Nachman St. 2) is located in the south of Jaffa. It is a very relaxed place; most of the guests like an alternative lifestyle and the bar offers good music and little snacks. Sometimes, the music comes from the guests themselves, the piano is just waiting for you to play it. Tel. 03-681.1205, https://www.facebook.com/shaffabar

8.2 Clubs

It is difficult to say where exactly the bar turns into a club. In Tel Aviv, they distinguish between bars and "mega bars": a bar with a dance floor. You can find many of them on YouTube, so you have an idea before you go.

North

1.) Shablul Jazz Club (Hangar 13, Tel Aviv port) is a must for all jazz lovers. While the site is only in Hebrew, but you still get an idea and can see when the concerts begin. Before or after the jazz, you can have a drink or something to eat in one of the bars and restaurants close by. However, the club also offers food. Tel. 03-546.1891, http://www.shabluljazz.com/schedule.php, info@shabluljazz.com

Center North

2.) House and techno lovers will like the underground club **Penguin** (43, Yehuda HaLevi St.) The club starts "late"; translation: afterhours. Open from Monday to Friday. Do not hesitate to go into the shabby entrance; as mentioned above, it is an underground club, https://www.facebook.com/PenguinTLV

3.) The **Valium Club** (Ben Yehuda St. 1), formerly "YaYa Club", is located in the Migdal high-rise building. The club caters to the mainstream clubbers; good music and great atmosphere are guaranteed. Although it is a night club, the Valium Club offers a nice menu. During hot summers, the visitors can enjoy a cooling breeze on the roof terrace. Open daily from 21.00 and on Shabbat as of 18.00. Sundays closed. http://valiumclub.com

South

4.) The star of the **Block Club** (157, Derech Shalma <Salameh>) is always the performing musician, not the bar. Many of the world's greatest DJs had their Israel debut in this club, http://www.block-club.com/ (Hebrew),

5.) **Ha'oman 17** (88, Abarbanel St.) belongs to the best in all of Israel and is also one of the biggest. On Thursdays and Fridays, this club is the meeting place for the international DJ world. The club is a landmark in Tel Aviv nightlife. Tel. 03-681.3636, https://www.facebook.com/haoman17telaviv (Hebrew).

9   Shopping

Tel Aviv lives a double life between the Near East and Europe and shopping is a special experience. The absence of a true oriental bazaar in Tel Aviv does not stop the locals from behaving as if. Everything is negotiable. It does not hurt to ask, e.g., if there is a discount if you pay cash or take more than one item. The more politely you ask, the better your chances. The following streets are worth strolling down to get an impression of the local offers. Every shop, but definitely every shopping center has its own security personnel. The little boutiques might not have anybody at their door, but most places are blocked by a security gate where your belongings are screened and bags opened. Israelis know the procedure and normally there are no lines.

1.) Allenby St.
During the 1920s, this was the most commercial street in Tel Aviv. Erwin Moses, son of the Jewish doctor and member of parliament Dr. Julius Moses, opened here in the 1930s the shop "The Gentleman", a haberdasher. Erwin Moses had immigrated to Palestine already in the early 1930s, but little is left from this period. Many houses seem to be only weeks away from collapsing but still stand like proud witnesses of golden times gone by. Vintage and second-hand shops, book merchants and shoe shops and somehow a little bit of everything can be found here.

2.) Bograshov St.
Unlike Allenby Street, on Bograshov, the focus is more on clothes, including second-hand and vintage.

3.) Dizengoff St.
For Jews from Berlin and Budapest, Dizengoff Street was a worthy substitute for the Kurfürstendamm. They had left their countries involuntarily and felt alien in the Near East, but not on Dizengoff. On Shabbat, they would come here for a walk, have a coffee in one of the many cafés and mingle with other Europeans. The Hebrew language even developed its own verb for this: le-hiz-dangef, to hang out in Dizengoff. The upper part (above Frishman St.) has always attracted customers with high spending power but in recent years, competition has shown up: Kikar HaMedina.

4.) Kikar HaMedina
It is the ultimate luxury address and as mentioned before, the competition of Northern Dizengoff. Many residents of the nearby Ramat Aviv (northern district of Tel Aviv) work in Israel's booming high-tech industry. These shops are not short of clients.

5.) Gan HaHashmal
Around the electricity garden (in Hebrew: *Gan HaHashmal*), former home of the first power plant, an interesting transformation has been taking place. The once neglected neighborhood is blossoming again and is now a must for fashion lovers: many little shops and showrooms from innovative young designers can be found here. Gan HaHashmal is surrounded by the streets of Yehuda HaLevy, HaRakevet, Menachem Begin and Allenby.

6.) Sheinkin St.
Sheinkin is legendary. Israel's leftwing scene lives here. The 1968 generation has gotten grey hair, but Sheinkin is still a relaxed place with alternative lifestyles, political discussions and an interesting mix of shops with Indian imports, incense sticks, organic food and informal clothes.

7.) Shabazi St.
Neve Tzedek is full of little treasures and some are hidden here in these little streets: fashion, jewelry and crafts and always a nice bistro or café in between.

8.) Tchernichovsky St.
This street is totally underestimated and hardly mentioned as a shopping destination. Tchernichovsky seems to be quiet and not commercial at all. Those who are ready for a surprise will discover little boutiques, and not only for women. At the corner of Allenby Street, you will find some nice bistros.

9.) Jaffa
Old Jaffa specializes in tourism while the streets around the flea market attract young designers who give the ancient place a new coat of paint. Next to the flea market, there are more second-hand-shops: antiques, silver, carpets, etc. Bargaining is a must; you are in the Near East. Inside the shops, it is much quieter but nowhere else in the city are Europe and Orient so close.

10.) HaTachana
1) The old HaTachana train station where once the Jaffa-Jerusalem line stopped was refurbished some years ago and has become a nice place for having a coffee, strolling through little boutiques, enjoying some good tapas and a glass of wine. The official tourist information can also be found on the compound where they also have a little souvenir shop. The Tachana is located at the southern end of Kaufman St., right next to the IDF Museum. Kaufman St./Mered St., http://www.hatachana.co.il.

11.) Sarona

is the new star of East Tel Aviv. Previously, the German Templars lived here autonomously from their own agriculture. The former Templar buildings are not only homes to shops but as well to cafés, bars and restaurants. Their original locations have been altered to form an ensemble with short distances. After a shopping day, nice food and a good glass of wine, in the shade of the Azrieli business center, are just some foot steps away.

9.1   Fashion

12.) The Israeli label **Frau Blau** was founded in 2002 by Helena Blaunstein and Philip Blau and soon became a major player in the Israeli fashion world. The design is fresh and modern, the special visual effects through print-ons are their trademark. David Elazar Str. 12, Tel. 03-560.1735, http://www.fraublau.com

13.)**Tanti Becky** is another star of the local fashion scene. Vintage, their own creations, imported clothes, jewelry and furniture… visiting Tanti Becky is fun! Bar Kochba St. 63, Tel. 03-525.5995, http://tantibecky.wordpress.com, http://www.facebook.com/tantibecky

14.) If you do not yet have any favorite pair of shoes, now you have no excuse anymore. At **Liebling Shoes**, you will find elegant leather shoes in a timeless design and high quality; limited edition. Bar Kochba St. 63, Tel. 03-525.1020, http://www.liebling-shoes.com.

9.2   Delicatessen

The local markets are usually a great place in the search of local delicatessen, especiallly Levinksi Street with its spice merchants (see chapter 9.4). This is were the locals go:

15.) **Chaim Rafael** (Levinski St. 36) has been a family-run business for three generations. Grandfather Rafael, a Greek Jew, came to Israel in 1958, after his liberation from Auschwitz. He started his delicatessen business at the current address. Today, Chaim Rafael's products can also be purchased online. http://www.haimrafael.co.il Hebrew), Tel. 03-682.6147.

9.3   Miscellaneous

Diamanten

The best way to find a serious diamond dealer is to go the Diamond Exchange in Ramat Gan, right inside the eastern city limit: 1, Jabotinsky St., the Harry

Oppenheimer Diamond Museum is also located here.

Judaica

Ben Yehuda St. is a good place to find a store for judaica. But there is one other shop that is worth being mentioned here:

16.) **Minzer** is a Judaica shop that is targeting frumm Jews rather than tourists. Once inside, you might feel reminded of those little Jewish Judaica merchants in New York where you can buy religious books, sidurim, a new talit, etc. In this secular city, a shop like Minzer is quite an exception. 112, Allenby St., Tel. 03-560.5635, binyamin81@neto.net.il, http://masoret.dpages.co.il (in Hebrew.)

Souvenirs

What is typically Israeli? Only you can say which impressions you want take home. If there is no more space in your suitcase for olive oil and salt from the Dead Sea, what about magnets with pictures from Tel Aviv (e.g., in HaTachana) or a t-shirt? Israelis love printed t-shirts and the supply of t-shirts in English and Hebrew is abundant. You can also embroider something with your name in Hebrew, but his requires at least two days of advanced planning.

17.) **Monograma** is well hidden in the little shopping center "London Mini-Store" on Ibn Gvirol. They embroider textiles with Hebrew letters and print photos on different things like cups, t-shirts and even flip-flops. 30, Ibn Gvirol St., Tel. 03-696.2950, monograma1@gmail.com, http://www.monograma.co.il (in Hebrew.)

9.4 Markets

The markets in Tel Aviv are a treasure trove for rarities from different cultures and religions. A multitude of odors and flavors as diverse as the Israeli society fuse with nostalgia. Jews have lived all over the world for centuries and here in the markets, you can find something from every corner of the world.

Flea Markets

1.) **Dizengoff Square** Tu. 14.00-20.00, Fr. 08.00-16.00

2.) **Shuk HaPishpeshim** (English: flea market) in Jaffa is the oldest and surely the most outstanding market of the city. Here in Jaffa where Judaism, Islam and Christianity meet, life is colorful and vibrant. Whether in the halls or outside, in this market you'll find kitsch, design, antiques, good junk– just everything. Do not forget to bargain! If not in Jaffa, where? Friday is the most crowded day of the week and some say also the most expensive. On the side streets, there is more to see and buy from local merchants and nobody has ever starved here. For quite a while now, this area has been considered "trendy"; young designers, restaurants, bars… and new neighbors are not changing the face of Old Jaffa. This is now the best time to come for a visit. Nobody knows how it will look years from now and whether this unique flair will survive. Yefet St./Oley Zion St., close to Clock Tower, Su.–Th. 10.00–18.00, Fr. 10.00–14.00.

Farmers' Markets
Before you go to the market, you might want to order a card called "**Shuk Bites**". With this card, you can taste local tapas from different booths at a fixed price. The card can be purchased online and will be delivered by email. http://www.shuktlv.co.il/en/

3.) The **Carmel Market** is located next to the Yemenite Quarter, a market with an outstanding and colorful selection of fresh vegetables and fruits. In the afternoon, the food gets cheaper before they close down. In between, you find little bistros with falafel, shavarma, fresh fish, spices, dried fruit and hot tea. From here, you can continue to the Yemenite Quarter where you are certain to find a nice little place for lunch.

4.) The everyday market is located inside the halls of the **port of Tel Aviv**, but every Friday, there is an additional farmers' market outside from 08.00-14.00. Sea view included! The prices are not as cheap as those at Carmel Market, but it has its very own flair and some products are even organic. The market is well worth a visit.

Afterwards, you can have a coffee or second breakfast next to the sea.

5.) The **port of Jaffa** has caught up with the port of Tel Aviv, and it now also offers an animated farmer's market. Wooden fisher boats and warehouses still remind the visitor of how busy and lively the Jaffa port used to be. Right here, in front of the aged warehouses, Jewish refugees had gotten off the ships on which they had managed to escape Nazi Europe. Close by, the renowned Jaffa Orange was packed and shipped. The farmer's market takes place on Friday mornings in the eastern part of the port, in Hangar 1. It is open from 09.00 to 14.00.

6.) The neighborhood around **Levinsky St.** is a bit rundown but full of life. When Jews were expelled from Arab countries in 1948 and came to Israel, many of them settled down in the south of the city. In the derelict houses between HaAliya and Herzl St. (many of them from the 1930s,) today you will find merchants for spices, dried fruits, olives and also for delicatessen items. Lunch time is the best time for a visit. You can nearly always taste the food before you buy. Friday is the busiest and most interesting day when people run from shop to shop before Shabbat.

Artisanry

7.) **Nachalat Binyamin**, the street of the "heirs of Theodor Herzl" (in Israel, Binyamin Herzl) is always good for a surprise. The audience is as diverse as the market itself: goldsmiths, potters, painters and other artists like street musicians, actors and fortune tellers exhibit their goods and services or simply themselves. There are plenty of opportunities to have a coffee and a snack in the neighboring cafés and bistros. Tu.–Fr. 10.00–16.30 starting at Allenby St./Nachalat Binyamin St., http://www.nachalatbinyamin.com

10 Accommodation

Finding a great hotel in Tel Aviv is not very difficult. The prices are in US-$ and any acceptable hotel starts at about $135 per night. Israel is a high-tech nation and an Internet connection is provided nearly everywhere you go. If you will require parking for your car, you should inquire about this with the hotel you are considering before you book. Parking space is very scarce in the city.

Consulting hotel websites is worth the while before booking even the flight. Many hotels offer discounts that are only good on certain days. Of course, you will also find major hotel chains like the Hilton or the Crowne Plaza. Cancellation policies vary with each hotel and each season, especially during the Jewish holidays. Most tourists are not aware of this. Many hotels do not accept cancellations later than 48 hours before arrival. During the High Holidays, it is customary for many hotels that the whole stay has to be paid in advance and cancellations are not accepted later than 10 days before arrival.

10.1 Hotels

Sadot Hotel, Ben Gurion Airport
http://www.atlas.co.il/sadot-hotel-tel-aviv
This airport hotel is not only a very comfortable solution when you have a night flight, this is the only Israeli hotel that has ever made it on the list of Expedia's best hotels of the world.

1.) The Varsano Hotel
Hevrat Shas, 16, http://thevarsano.com
The Varsano offers exceptional suites in a historic area. Close to the old Jaffa train station (tachana), this hotel hides behind a little wooden door in the middle of the villagey Neve Tzedek while still being situated in the center of buzzing Tel Aviv. Cut off the outer world and have an unforgettable stay in the stylish and modern suites.

2.) Brown TLV
Kalisher St 25, http://www.browntlv.com
This hotel opened end of 2010 and was soon renowned for its modern and elegant design together with nice features like iPod charging stations in the rooms. The in-house wellness offerings are far above average as is the charming roof terrace. A very good value for the money! The hotel is located in the very north of Neve Tzedek, a very lively part of Tel Aviv. The Yemenite Quarter as well as the Rothschild Boulevard can be reached by foot.

3.) **The Rothschild Hotel**

Rothschild Blvd. 96, http://www.rothschild-hotel.co.il

Every Tel Avivi knows the emblematic building on Rothschild Boulevard, with the singers on the balcony. This is the center of the 1930s Tel Aviv, locally known as "the heart" of the White City (*ha lev*, or *lev ha ir* for "heart of the city"). The house is a typical representative of the international style and offers an authentic Tel Aviv feeling . The new hotel is proud of its ecological approach; much emphasis is placed on recycling and all products (shower gels, etc.) come from local companies. The rooms are elegantly furnished and designed with herringbone parquett flooring.

4.) **The Diaghilev**, LIVE ART Boutique Hotel)

Mazeh St. 56, http://www.diaghilev.co.il

As the name suggests, this hotel is all about art. Every single one of the suites is a little art gallery of its own. The hotel is only one block away from famous Rothschild Boulevard and you can reach many sites by foot. This building in the International Style was built in 1934 by architects Josef & Ze'ev Berlin and served as the first headquarters of the newspaper Hearts that still exists today.

5.) **Center Chic Hotel**

Zamenhoff St. 2, http://www.atlas.co.il/centr-hotel-tel-aviv

It is hardly possible to be "more Tel Aviv" than this hotel. Breakfast is served in the Cinema Hotel on Dizengoff Square, a so-called "Bauhaus building" that transports the guest to the bygone era of the 1930s, the time of the city's first architectural boom. With free bikes from the hotel, it is easy to explore the city. Later, you can come back for tea time on the roof terrace.

6.) **Esther Cinema Hotel**

Zamenhoff St. 1, http://www.atlas.co.il/cinema-hotel-tel-aviv

Like being in a movie! The Cinema Hotel is the "big brother" of the Center Chic Hotel and a must for cineastes. The architects Yehuda & Raphael built it in 1939 in the "International Style" of the 1930s. Before it became a hotel, i used to be home to the Esther Cinema which is the theme of the whole building: all decoration is movie-related.

7.) Townhouse Tel Aviv
Yavne St. 32, http://www.townhousetelaviv.com
The hotel combines modern design with comfort. Guests will enjoy all the benefits of a high hotel standard while feel like living like a local. The public areas are cozy like a private living room. During the day, you will be served free tea, coffee and biscuits. Breakfast is prepared by the renowned Café Bakery 29.

8.) The Rothschild 71
Rothschild Blvd. 71, http://www.the-rothschild.com
The hotel is located in an International Style building from 1934. The Rothschhild 71 offers modern suites and studios with first-class service and top fit out and amenities (e.g. Nespresso machine, L'Occitane products in the bathroom, etc.). Guest will enjoy their breakfast in the café-restaurant CANTINA, which is located on the ground floor.

9.) Shalom Hotel & Relax Tel Aviv
HaYarkon St 216, http://www.atlas.co.il/shalom-hotel-tel-aviv.
Shalom & Relax. Nomen est omen: Welcome to the start of your holiday! In the neighborhood of the marina as well as other upper-class hotels like Hilton, Crowne Plaza, etc., and the exclusive shops of the Northern Dizengoff. The roof top offers a wonderful view and a nice terrace.

10.) Hotel Montefiore
Montefiore St 36, http://www.hotelmontefiore.co.il
This exclusive little boutique hotel hides in the heart of Tel Aviv. The building is from 1922 and shows the typical Eclectic Style from this period. This neighborhood was the first of the young Tel Aviv (Achuzat Beit.) Strategically located between Rothschild Boulevard, Sheinkin Street and the Yemenite Quarter, you can walk anywhere from here. The style of the rooms is very welcoming in warm colors and decorated with works from young Israeli artists. Do not miss the cuisine of the hotel's restaurant!

11.) Arbel Hotel Apartment
Hulda Street 11, http://www.israelapartment.com
This exclusive little boutique hotel hides in the heart of Tel Aviv. The building is from 1922 and shows the typical Eclectic Style from this period. This neighborhood was the first of the young Tel Aviv (Achuzat Beit.) Strategically located between Rothschild Boulevard, Sheinkin Street and the Yemenite Quarter, you can walk

anywhere from here. The style of the rooms is very welcoming in warm colors and decorated with works from young Israeli artists. Do not miss the cuisine of the hotel's restaurant!

10.2 Hostels

If a hotel is just not right for your budget or preference, you might want to consider a hostel where you can spend the night for about $25. Ear plugs should be part of your basic equipment. Most of the hostels offer a kitchen you can use and free Wi-Fi Internet. The breakfast is generally not worth mentioning (except for the Gordon Inn.) They can all be booked via the established online portals, but the following two addresses are worth being mentioned:

12.) **Old Jaffa Hostel**, Oley Zion St 8, Jaffa
This colorfully decorated hostel is legendary, and the atmosphere is a very authentic reflection of the busy and diverse life in Jaffa. The roof terrace is the place to have coffee in the morning, or – if you wish – the place where you find a hammock for the night.

13.) **Chef Hostel Montefiore**, Montefiore St. 19
The hostel is being operated by a local family. It is consistently voted the best hostel in Tel Aviv and there is a reason for it: the moment you step in, you become part of the family. They charge a bit more than the other hostels, but this extra dollar is well invested. The modern place offers the guests an open kitchen for joined cooking and a charming terrace.